"Some authors do a great job but they leave us without any hope or solutions to the problem. The Dunhams' book is an honest and personal account of their own struggle while also offering practical and biblical ways of reframing that struggle with insights and hope that were forged in the trenches of failure and longing for real change. Those who have tried and failed before won't be crushed by the gentle, humble, and gracious tone that characterizes the hearts of David and Krista. I expect this book will be a beacon of hope in the dark struggle of eating disorders."

Brad Bigney, Pastor of Grace Fellowship, Florence, KY; certified ACBC counselor; conference speaker; author of *Gospel Treason*

"*Table for Two* by David and Krista Dunham is a refreshingly honest book with a refreshingly unique perspective. David and Krista coauthor as a couple who have walked through an eating disorder—one as a person reaching out for help, the other as a helper-in-training. As they invite you into their journey, you'll learn from a biblical perspective the underlying issues related to eating disorders, and you'll learn how to compassionately and competently help those working through this issue."

Bob Kellemen, Academic Dean and Professor of Biblical Counseling at Faith Bible Seminary; author of *Gospel-Centered Marriage Counseling* and *Gospel-Centered Family Counseling*

"As biblical counseling continues to grow and mature, it has needed to address issues such as eating disorders with a level of competence and care that befits the complexity of the problem it represents. David and Krista Dunham have skillfully and compassionately done exactly that. If you are looking for a resource that addresses eating disorders with humility, compassion, and grace, look no further than this book!"

Jonathan D. Holmes, Pastor of Counseling, Parkside Church; executive director, Fieldstone Counseling

"David and Krista Dunham have written a much-needed resource for those counseling or those struggling with disordered eating. It is a story of how a couple struggles with this complex issue, how they fail and then find help and hope through a biblical approach and process of healing. They illustrate the common path of shame, isolation, secrecy, and control that often accompanies eating disorders. What's unique to this book is how they navigated this as a couple and how Krista finally got to the heart of the issue through biblical counsel. I highly recommend this book for those struggling with eating issues and those who love and counsel them."

Garrett Higbee, Pastor of Biblical Soul Care, Harvest Church North Indianapolis; president, Soul Care Consulting

"What an excellent contribution to the literature on eating disorders! Many silently fight this battle alone and unknown, adding shame and despair to their struggles. And many more friends, family, and helpers feel desperately incapable to help, not even knowing where to start. David and Krista apply their personal experiences to wisely exhort, educate, and encourage both the person struggling with an eating disorder as well as the one committed to help. I've already recommended this book to clients."

Greg Wilson, LPC Supervisor, Lead Counselor at Soul Care Associates

"I've battled against disordered eating in the past, so I know that change is no simplistic equation. Yet *Table for Two* reminds me that no matter how perplexing our problems are, God's Word is sufficient to comfort, counsel, and persevere us through them. If you're looking to navigate the many complexities of disordered eating from a holistic, biblical perspective, I commend David and Krista as trustworthy guides."

Christine Chappell, Author of *Help! I've Been Diagnosed with a Mental Disorder, Help! My Teen is Depressed, Clean Home, Messy Heart, and Change for Overwhelmed Moms;* outreach director and podcast host, Institute for Biblical Counseling & Discipleship (IBCD)

"*Table for Two* gives voice to the agonizing experience of living with an eating disorder. With honest transparency and a hope-filled understanding of the path forward, this book provides biblical avenues for helpful conversations and practical direction toward lasting recovery. As a biblical and clinical counselor, I am relieved to know a resource like this finally exists! Their story delivers biblical direction that steers clear of quick-fix answers or simplistic advice and instead offers hope to both the sufferer and the helper."

Eliza Huie, LCPC; author of *Raising Kids in a Screen-Saturated World, Raising Teens in a Hyper-Sexualized World,* and *The Whole Life: 52 Weeks of Biblical Self-Care*

"As biblical counseling further develops from a movement to a discipline, it needs more issue-specific books providing a biblical framework to address specific troubles in human experience. David and Krista have provided such a book, helping us further stretch toward competency on the vital issue of eating disorders."

Jeremy Pierre, Author of *The Dynamic Heart in Daily Life*; Lawrence & Charlotte Hoover Associate Professor of Biblical Counseling; chair, Department of Biblical Counseling & Family Ministry, The Southern Baptist Theological Seminary

"When I go looking for help and direction in dealing with truly difficult problems, I'm always interested in those who have been there and found the way out. In the arena of eating disorders, *Table for Two* is compelling testimony of a couple who did just that. This book is full of help for the struggler and those who love them. The authors point the reader to the wealth of wisdom to be found when counseling from the Scriptures and the importance of good medical care in the process. Even the title is helpful, as it points the reader to the truth that eating disorders are rarely conquered alone. *Table for Two* will be an encouragement to many and a good resource in counseling."

Charles D. Hodges, Jr., MD, Family Physician, Indianapolis, IN; executive director, Vision of Hope, Residential Treatment Facility for Women, Lafayette, IN

"In *Table for Two*, David and Krista Dunham offer readers the healing balm of the gospel, applying it to the struggle of disordered eating. Compassionate, practical, and wise, the Dunhams' words are underscored by their own testimonies as they live in the hope they now extend—both to those who suffer and to those who help."

Hannah Anderson, Author of *Humble Roots: How Humility Grounds and Nourishes Your Soul*

"I appreciate David and Krista's patient, supportive approach. You can tell he is as content to be a patient shepherd on a hard journey as he is excited about the destination—overcoming an eating disorder with biblical guidance. When you're stuck in a life-dominating pattern, this demeanor is important. If you're stuck, you can trust David and Krista's book to provide patient guidance. If you're walking alongside someone who is stuck, you can trust *Table for Two* to help you pace your care and model the tone of the Good Shepherd. I have come to trust not only the content of David and Krista's counsel, but also the tenderness with which they do counseling. I think you will too."

Brad Hambrick, Pastor of Counseling at The Summit Church; assistant professor of Biblical Counseling, Southeastern Baptist Theological Seminary; general editor for *Becoming a Church that Cares Well for the Abused*

TABLE FOR TWO

BIBLICAL COUNSEL FOR EATING DISORDERS

David and Krista Dunham

newgrowthpress.com

New Growth Press, Greensboro, NC 27404
newgrowthpress.com
Copyright © 2021 by David and Krista Dunham

Unless otherwise indicated, Scripture quotations are taken from *The Holy Bible, English Standard Version*®. Copyright © 2000; 2001 by Crossway Bibles, a division of Good News Publishers. Used by permission. All rights reserved.

Scripture references marked NIV are taken from THE HOLY BIBLE, NEW INTERNATIONAL VERSION®, NIV® Copyright © 1973, 1978, 1984, 2011 by Biblica, Inc.® Used by permission. All rights reserved worldwide.

Cover Design: Faceout Books, faceoutstudio.com
Interior Design and Typesetting: Gretchen Logterman

ISBN: 978-1-64507-074-0 (Print)
ISBN: 978-1-64507-091-7 (eBook)

Library of Congress Cataloging-in-Publication Data on file

Names: Dunham, David R., author. | Duham, Krista, author.
Title: Table for two : biblical counsel for eating disorders / David and Krista Duham.
Description: Greensboro : New Growth Press, [2021] | "Scripture quotations are taken from The Holy Bible, English Standard Version Copyright, 2000; 2001 by Crossway Bibles, a division of Good News Publishers." | Includes bibliographical references. | Summary: "In this unique book, David and Krista Dunham share their journey through her eating disorder"-- Provided by publisher.
Identifiers: LCCN 2020038226 (print) | LCCN 2020038227 (ebook) | ISBN 9781645070740 (print) | ISBN 9781645070917 (ebook)
Subjects: LCSH: Eating disorders--Patients--Religious life. | Eating disorders--Religious aspects--Christianity. | Eating disorders--Patients--Pastoral counseling of.
Classification: LCC BV4910.35 .D96 2021 (print) | LCC BV4910.35 (ebook) | DDC 248.8/627--dc23
LC record available at https://lccn.loc.gov/2020038226
LC ebook record available at https://lccn.loc.gov/2020038227

Printed in the United States of America

28 27 26 25 24 23 22 21   1 2 3 4 5

We would like to dedicate this book to two dear friends who have given us countless words of encouragement, counsel, and correction. They have been champions of our writing, and we are thankful to God for their role in our lives and in seeing this book completed.

To Denise Hardy and Diana Smith—thank you.

Contents

Introduction 1

Chapter 1: Understanding an Eating Disorder 11
Chapter 2: Understanding Your Role and
               Embracing the Process of Change 25
Chapter 3: Understanding Our Motives 43
Chapter 4: Dealing with Core Issues 59
Chapter 5: Identity 83
Chapter 6: Restructuring Your Life for Change 93
Chapter 7: Working Together toward Healing 113
Appendix A: Compulsive Exercise Evaluation 123
Appendix B: Choosing a Good Counselor 127
Appendix C: Resources for Continued Study 131

Endnotes 133

Introduction

Krista's Story

Imagine that you're drowning in the ocean at night. Hours have passed since the sun disappeared over the horizon. The sky is dark. As you slip beneath the waves, you realize that the vast space beneath the ocean surface is even darker. You fight to keep your head above the crashing surf, but one heavy blow after another sends you swirling into the expanse below. The air escapes from your lungs, and you begin to sink. As you are falling, you feel the urgency to grasp for the surface. The dire need for oxygen gives you a rush of adrenaline, but as you have twisted and turned in the water, you have lost all sense of direction. As time passes you start to lose hope. Even if you had any energy left to push toward the surface, you have no idea which way to swim. You will drown if no one comes to your rescue.

And then, just when you think you have breathed your last breath, a strong arm wraps around you in the depths of your struggle and pulls you above the ocean waves. As you break the surface, your lungs involuntarily devour as much air as they can hold and your body calms as the urgency for breath is no longer a demand. Though you can't even see the face of the one who is holding you, you rest in the general security of knowing you are not alone anymore. When you are finally pulled up to the rescue boat, you lie back and close your eyes, allowing a relieved laugh to escape from your exhausted lungs. "Hey," the person says, "are you okay? I'm here to help." Those are the best words you have heard in your life, because you know you would have never made it out of the water alive without help.

There was part of me that knew right away I needed help. Within the first month of experiencing my disturbing food behavior at age eighteen, I sat down and wrote my boyfriend (now husband) a letter. I never sent it but instead chose to read it immediately to him over the phone. I am surprised now at how frankly I expressed my experiences to him.

"I eat hardly anything in front of people, but then, when no one is around, I eat so much that I make myself sick. I maintain my weight by working out obsessively, and there is hardly a moment of the day that goes by that I don't think about my weight or food or calories. I've been skipping meals to punish myself for eating too much the day before." Even in reading these words out loud, I could tell that it was all very raw.

"I'm really scared of what I'm doing to myself, but I don't know how to stop."

I don't remember any of the conversation that followed that big admission, but I do remember that David still called me the next day. I remember that he still wanted to go on a date with me when we were both home from college on Christmas break. He stuck around, and that's what I needed. If we could go back in time, there are many things we would both do differently (hence the writing of this book), but he put a hand out and said "I'm here to help," and I'm forever grateful that he did.

Maybe you've picked up this book because you are in a similar situation, desperate for help but with no clue where to turn. You may know you have a problem, but you feel overwhelmed by what it would mean to try to get better. Maybe you have recognized the signs, maybe someone has confronted you, or maybe you are done facing the consequences. Perhaps you've even asked someone for help but haven't seen anything develop from that conversation. Chances are, the person you talked to is confused and lost as well and may need some guidance. Whether you are a helper or a sufferer, for most people, the path to recovery from an eating disorder is brand-new territory. My husband and I have walked the road to recovery together, and we hope to help you find the way. We aim to help you identify potential motives that drive an eating disorder, navigate triggers, and find hope and healing in God. We aim especially to help you talk about these issues, bring them to the light, and address them with God's Word.

David's Story

I don't remember exactly what I thought when Krista first told me that she had an eating disorder. We were relatively young, and I was immature. I am sure my thoughts were selfish. (*This is going to mess up my life. Why does my future wife have to struggle with this?*) Whatever my thoughts, I at least knew I needed to attempt to be helpful, but I honestly didn't know where to begin. In truth, Krista needed help, and I needed help learning to be a helper.

I am a biblical counselor by profession and training. Counseling is what I do every day, but when I first learned of Krista's struggle I was a college student. I had never considered that I might need to learn how to be helpful. Many of us just think we are, or we reduce "help" to offering rudimentary spiritual guidance ("Just pray about it," "Think positively," "Love yourself more," "Confess and repent of your sin," etc.). Thinking we have then imparted wisdom, we pat ourselves on the back for being so considerate. At other times we put the entire burden on the suffering person to tell us what they need. Many times during that first year of marriage I asked my wife, "What can I do to help you?" She did not know the answer, and it put all the pressure on her. I meant well, but I hadn't taken the time to learn how to help her. Looking back, I wish I had found resources that could have guided me in a biblically faithful way through the nature of an eating disorder, the common experiences and frustrations of those who suffer, and the ways in which I could have been more helpful. Since then I have become a counselor and have learned a lot about counseling—and about counseling people with eating disorders in particular. This book reflects much of what I needed to know back then.

Maybe you picked this book up because you are in that same role of helper. Your spouse, child, parent, or friend has an eating disorder. Maybe they've told you, or maybe you just see all the signs, but either way you know there's something wrong and you want to help. Maybe, however, you simply don't know what to do. How can someone who has never had an eating disorder really be helpful? Even a helper who has recovered or is recovering from an eating disorder may not be a trained counselor, or a dietician, or medical doctor. What can you say? What can you do? Where do you even begin? This book is written for you, friend. It is intended to both encourage and educate. It is designed to give you some basic tools, point you in the right direction, and give you exercises that you can work on with your loved one. It is a book that can help you be a helper.

We All Need Help

Whether we are a sufferer or a helper or both we all need someone to walk alongside us. Many of us have been taught to believe that we are independent, autonomous, and self-sufficient individuals. We don't need anyone else. Only weak people ask for help. This mindset can often be found in the recovery community too. We (David and Krista) both work with addicted individuals in our church-based recovery program and we often find that the common phrase among addicts of various stripes is, "I need to do this for myself, by myself." But self-sufficiency keeps individuals stuck. The Bible tells us that we desperately need one another.

Ecclesiastes communicates our need for one another clearly and powerfully:

Two are better than one, because they have a good return for their labor: If either of them falls down, one can help the other up. But pity anyone who falls and has no one to help them up. Also, if two lie down together, they will keep warm. But how can one keep warm alone? Though one may be overpowered, two can defend themselves. A cord of three strands is not quickly broken. (Ecclesiastes 4:9–12 NIV)

The passage uses two examples to help illustrate the value of mutual support. The first is with regard to work. When two work together their work is easier, they are able to accomplish more, and, significantly, if one falls, a faithful friend will be there to lend a hand. The second example points to protection. On a cold night, lying close together would keep each person warmer than simply sleeping alone. Likewise, while one person alone might not be able to resist an enemy, two together can withstand him. The passage ends, however, with a transition; this two-fold help turns into a "cord of three strands." In all recovery, this third person is vital to the process of change. Jesus Christ is our true help, and his empowering grace makes all the difference. As you and your companion seek to address the eating disorder together, you will want to regularly look to Christ for the additional help you need. Protection happens in communion with others and with Christ, not in isolation.

Eating disorders thrive in isolation. Shame, guilt, fear of exposure, and anxiety over food and eating can become so intense that those who suffer simply shrink their world until they are utterly alone. They may go to work, go to the gym, go to the store, but such activities may happen amidst a total lack of deep interpersonal connection. "Pity anyone who falls and has no one to help them up!" Without friends, helpers, counselors, and advocates, recovery will never happen. Eating disorders, of which there are various types, covering a wide spectrum of unhealthy relations to food and eating (including both binging and restrictive behaviors) are serious, often life-threatening issues. It's important to recognize the urgent need for help and support in confronting these issues.

In preparing to write this book, I (Krista) pulled out some of my old journals. In many of my early entries I sounded optimistic. I sounded sure of my faith. I sounded like I was getting better and almost like it was silly for me to have ever thought that there was anything wrong.

> "I have changed so much over the last month!"
> "I still slip up every once in a while . . . but it feels different this time."
> "I've really been praying that God will get me through this and I really trust him this time."

In these repeated phrases, however, I noticed a major inconsistency. In retrospect, I can see that the story of my actual experience did not fully line up with the story I had written in my journal. Those sentences were written ten years before I actually reached the point of being fully recovered from my eating disorder. Although I was on the path to recovery back then, it turned out to be longer than I realized in the moment and harder than I was able to deal with on my own. Along the way, there was a recurring pattern: I constantly thought I was doing better than I really was. On my own, I consistently tried to get better, and I consistently failed. I was blind to what was truly happening in my struggle and I needed someone to point that out to me. I was running in circles because my own myopic tendency was to tell myself I was doing okay when it was obvious that I wasn't. My pride wanted to convince me that I was fine without help, but truthfully, no one can sustain the fight against an eating disorder on their own. The temptation, seduction, and deception of an eating disorder will often "overpower" one who is alone, but with a friend and advocate you can withstand.

The New Testament echoes this need of mutual support in the fight against sin. In his letter to the Galatians, Paul writes:

Brothers, if anyone is caught in any transgression, you who are spiritual should restore him in a spirit of gentleness. Keep watch on yourself, lest you too be tempted. Bear one another's burdens, and so fulfill the law of Christ. For if anyone thinks he is something, when he is nothing, he deceives himself. (Galatians 6:1–3)

While Ecclesiastes emphasizes the importance of community for those struggling, the emphasis in Galatians is for helpers to actively come alongside those who struggle. The crux of the passage is the command to "bear one another's burdens, and so fulfill the law of Christ" (v. 2). But this directive is to be profoundly inflected by a posture of compassion, responsibility, and humility.

The section begins by discussing those who are "caught" in sin and encourages helpers to have genuine compassion for those who struggle. That word "caught" is an important word for thinking about the nature of eating disorders. The text is not just discussing those who sin, but those who are "caught" in sin's snare, in bondage, enslaved, even surprised or caught unaware. In the New Testament, "sin" is not simply human action; it is a power that stands opposed to God and deceives and enslaves humanity (Romans 7:7–8:1). This struggle against the dark force of sin is a struggle for liberation. Our brothers and sisters struggling with eating disorders did not plan to become enslaved. But one of the principal powers of an enslaving master is making those who are captive feel like they are powerless. In Romans 6, Paul speaks of "letting sin reign" and of "sin reigning." Ed Welch echoes this biblical idea that addictions—including habitual patterns of disordered eating—involve us in a "voluntary slavery." [1] Addictive habits are both the choices we make and the habits that become enslaving. Part of the power of habits is that, once they are developed, we don't have to think intentionally about doing those things; they just come automatically. Breaking a habit, then, is not simply about choosing to stop. It's about being set free from slavery.

Paul urges, then, that those who are "spiritual" should provide aid (v.1). In such scenarios, Paul tells us, those who are spiritually mature are to "restore" such believers (v.1). That means that we have a responsibility to care for those in bondage. Restoration in each case is going to look different, and it will involve multiple layers of interaction and activity. But notice in verse 2 that it also involves bearing one another's burdens. Recovering does not happen in isolation. It requires a community to help bear some of the load, to give comfort, support, challenge, assistance, and practical counsel. It involves walking alongside somebody for the long haul and not giving up on them every time they fall off the wagon. Helping one another fight temptation, avoid places of temptation, restructure a life, and rebuild broken relationships is how we work to "restore" a brother or sister. This is the type of restoration that will be described throughout the course of this book—how to reach out for this help if you suffer from an eating disorder, and how to begin to offer this care if you are a loved one looking to help.

While urging helpers to help, Paul warns that they must be humble (v.3). The Galatian church was full of false teachers who were claiming to be super spiritual. Paul rebukes such attitudes of superiority. In essence, if you think you're better than those "caught in any transgression," think again. Godly helpers recognize that we are all, at one level or another, in recovery. We are all plagued in various ways by our own weaknesses, and we are all in need of spiritual help and assistance from our brothers and sisters. You might be in the helper role right now, but you've been in need of help in the past, and you will be in need of help again in the future. Helpers need to guard their own hearts from a sort of spiritual pride that elevates them above those whose lives appear messier, whose sins seem more serious, and whose brokenness seems more frustrating. Such pride is sin and in order to be helpful, you will need to put off arrogance and put on humility in its place (Colossians 3:12). But the fact remains that in the family of God, we are called and empowered to help one another, sharing the mind of the one who came to bring us freedom from bondage (Philippians 2:1–11; Colossians 1:13).

We all need help. If you are presently struggling with an eating disorder, this book is designed to help you ask for such help. It will assist you in acquiring the right kind of help. Use it to focus your requests and conversations. If you are a helper, this book will provide you some basic education on eating disorders and assist you in focusing your help in meaningful ways. We will walk readers through several key components of the helping process. That process begins with education, moves to self-evaluation, and finally concludes with a restructuring plan. Each chapter will include sections by both David and Krista. Krista will be sharing her own experiences with an eating disorder, describing her thoughts, her fears, her behaviors, and her needs. Her experience is not intended to represent everyone's experience, but there may be still much that you can learn from her even if your story doesn't match hers. David will write from a helper standpoint, both as Krista's husband in the midst of her struggle, and as a biblical counselor. Sufferers and helpers can read the book together, discussing what they learned from the chapters. Each chapter will conclude with an interactive exercise designed to help you engage the principles of the chapter together. In this way we hope that the book will be an active helping tool, giving you the chance to actually practice what you learn.

A Word of Caution

Before jumping into this book, let us urge you to consider these important disclaimers and cautions.

First, this book should not be used in place of competent counseling. It is a tool, but a competent counselor is invaluable to your progress (see appendix B).

Second, it is vitally important that you consult a dietician if you are struggling with an eating disorder. Depending on what you have been doing, and how long you have been doing it, your life may be in jeopardy. The principles in this book will be helpful to you, but they cannot help you if you are dead. To find a dietician near you who specializes in eating disorder treatment, visit the website of NEDA, the National Eating Disorders Association (https://www.nationaleatingdisorders.org/).

Third, this book is designed to be read with a helper. If you are suffering from an eating disorder, invite a trusted friend, a parent, or another loved one to walk through these chapters with you.

CHAPTER 1

Understanding an Eating Disorder

Understanding an eating disorder can be difficult for those who have never experienced it. What does it mean to struggle with eating, or to be anxious about food? Understanding the basics of an eating disorder can go a long way in assisting both helpers and sufferers to navigate the problem.

We can understand issues like this from two important and complementary perspectives. On the one hand we can learn the facts. It's important to gather information on what an eating disorder is, the symptoms, long-term damage, and common motivations. As a counselor I (David) know about these dynamics, and I hope to share insight on these matters. But there is another type of insight that is useful for understanding eating disorders—the experiential insight. In this chapter Krista will share her own experience with an eating disorder and describe how it developed and how it impacted her. Both insights will be valuable to sufferer and helper.

It's important to keep in mind, as we begin, that we face these issues as people made by God and redeemed by Christ. This means God has created our bodies and wants to help us become good stewards of his created work. Christ has redeemed us, and we are his, called to glorify him with our bodies (1 Corinthians 6:19–20).

Krista's Story

I didn't plan to have an eating disorder. I didn't randomly get up one morning and determine that I wasn't going to eat anymore. I didn't enjoy eating all the food in my cabinets until my stomach hurt. I didn't want to exercise until 3:00 am. I didn't make any resolutions to start weighing myself obsessively. And I didn't find it particularly productive to keep meticulous notebooks of all the calories I had eaten. It all felt like it came out of nowhere. It felt like it was beyond my control. At first it felt intrusive, but gradually it became normal and I felt like there was nothing I could do to stop it.

As a Christian, it frustrated me that knowing, loving, and following God hadn't completely protected me from succumbing to an eating disorder. I had become a believer when I was six years old and had grown in the knowledge of God. I had seen examples of fruit in my life that assured me that I was certainly a child of God. I loved the Bible and wanted to apply it to my life. But I still developed an eating disorder. I was frustrated by this until I realized that even Christians can be influenced by the sin and suffering of the world. There are circumstances we experience, such as trauma or abuse, that happen because we live in a sin-cursed world. And not only that, but as Christians, we can still choose sinful responses. I had specifically allowed some of my personal characteristics and choices to be left unchecked, which led to sinful patterns of thought and action. I needed help applying the Word of God to those areas of my life.

As a child, I liked everything to be perfect. My outfits always had to match, and I had to find the right picture to color in my coloring book before I could lift a crayon. When it came to games, I had to make sure I could perfectly perform on my first attempt, so I watched everyone else do it until I was sure I could do it the best. In school I needed perfect attendance and straight As. In sports I had to get first place. I liked winning and achieving. I liked working hard and seeing my efforts pay off. And for most of my childhood that system worked for me without any obvious negative impact.

Upon entering middle school, my self-confidence dwindled, and I slipped into the steady, easy flow of trying to please my classmates. As I became aware that I couldn't always control what other people thought of me, my well-structured view of life began to crumble. I had always thought the best of people, but this new revelation about the uncontrollable motives of others caused my strong, positive attitude to fall apart and revealed an untrusting skepticism that marred my view of relationships in general. If I couldn't control others, if they were always going to be unpredictable, then I was going to keep them at a distance. Pleasing others became a frustrating goal that was always just out of my reach. My thoughts became obsessed with never being pretty enough, smart enough, or popular enough. I felt empty and so I filled in the gaps by studying more and working harder. Relationships became risky and unstable because I couldn't control them. Achievement became the Band-Aid solution that I used to cover over the anxieties I had about relationships. I felt awkward and ill equipped at making conversations. Achievement gave me confidence. I felt like a failure at keeping and maintaining relationships. Achievement made me feel successful. I didn't know how to relate to people. Achievement made me popular. My dad recognized me when I scored the most points. My grandparents gave me attention when I got straight As. My mom got excited when I sang a solo well. My friends gave me gifts when I got the star role in the school play. And my classmates cheered when I won a race. But achievement was only a ruse. It only made me *feel* like I was okay. My friends and family weren't doing anything wrong, but I began interpreting things in a wrong way. Their affirmations became my identity. Achievement was safe, and it made me feel good. Healthy relationships were tiresome, difficult, and unsafe. So I stuck to what was easier.

I tied my worth to my achievements. I was one of the smartest students in my class; I was the star of the school musical; I got first place in all my track races. It seemed that everything I put my mind to, if I worked hard enough, I could achieve success and recognition. By all outward appearances I was winning at life. But during this time, my mind went to some very sinister places. I desperately wanted to be somewhere else and to be someone else. Everything I was doing was not good enough for me. Trophies and medals didn't squelch the gnawing loneliness that swept over me when I laid my head on my pillow at night. Awards and status could never heal the gaping wound of insecurity I felt around other people. As I sank deeper, my heart longed more and more for the approval of my peers. I just wanted to fit in. I questioned myself over every word I planned to say. Many times I just didn't say anything at all. I beat myself up for months over forgetting a line in the school play or getting second place in a race or tripping in front of an upperclassman. I called myself stupid and ugly and useless and unlovable. I kept everyone at a distance because I was so afraid they would see me mess up. I used perfectionism as a shield. I wanted to protect myself against the pain of being vulnerable and the discomfort of receiving criticism. It hurt to be imperfect, and I desired to avoid that at all cost. I continued to think that perfection was not only attainable, but also the only standard by which I could ever approve of myself. I failed to see the grace and forgiveness that came from giving up my desire to judge myself. I was never meant to be the judge of perfection— only God can do that. And in his courtroom, I will always have a perfect advocate, Jesus Christ, who stands in my place and who was completely perfect on my behalf so that I don't have to be. Without this truth, I continued to believe that as long as I didn't obtain my idea of perfection, I was worthless. As long as I was still making mistakes, I was nothing.

As high school came to a close, I imagined that college was my time to find freedom from all of the negative feelings I had been pushing down. I could start over and be a new person, a person who wasn't afraid of making mistakes and who could try new things without fear of the consequences. I got the haircut I had always wanted but was afraid of trying. I wore clothes that I had always wanted to wear but had been afraid to because of what my friends would think. I thought I was doing well with overcoming my perfectionism. But college life brought unique choices and challenges that I didn't have the resources to navigate. And as I tried to figure out these issues, I realized that my destructive thought patterns were still chained to me. Like many other college students, I was faced with what felt like an insurmountable number of choices. What would I study? What activities would I be involved in? Who would my new friends be? When would I say yes? When would I say no? How much money would I spend? How would I spend my free time? When would I study? I had a million decisions to make but, to me, each one of them had to be made perfectly. I still wanted everyone to approve of me.

College meant a more sedentary lifestyle, and eating a lot of junk food—cookies, ice cream, and pizza. Of course I gained about fifteen pounds over the first semester of my freshman year. It's a common occurrence affectionately referred to as "the freshman fifteen." But it didn't feel common to me. I felt as if I were the only one. I felt out of control. I felt ugly. I felt imperfect. I felt worthless.

These thoughts carried on into my sophomore year. As I drove home after the first semester of my sophomore year, my head was swirling with self-destroying thoughts. *Your friends don't really like you. You are alone and that's how you deserve to be. You are stupid for choosing education as your major. You shouldn't have even gone to college.* I spent the three-hour drive home for Christmas mentally ripping every part of my life to shreds. My thoughts were abruptly halted, however, when my SUV slipped on a patch of ice, slid out of control and spun around. I instinctively pushed the brakes as hard as I could and instead of stopping, the top-heavy car flipped and skidded upside down across the guardrail, crushing the roof and busting out the back windows. Though I couldn't see anything around me, I knew where I was in my route and I pictured the endlessly deep ravine that awaited me on the other side. I closed my eyes and braced myself for inevitable death, but the car mysteriously landed with all four tires back on the road. I walked away without a scratch.

I traveled back to school after the holiday still shaken from the trauma I had experienced. My mind was in a constant buzz trying to understand what had happened. I began to come to grips with the fact that life and death are out of my control. I could have died that day, but I had no control over it either way. Instead of being thankful for my life, I began grasping at any control I could get my hands on. Exercise was my first vice. I spent hours in the gym, often skipping classes to use the elliptical. I spent more time in the weight room than I did with my friends. The feeling of control I got from dropping seconds off my mile time wasn't enough, so I then started restricting my diet. I nibbled on salads, banned all sugared beverages, said no to all desserts, and skipped meals. I finally felt strong and in control. I convinced myself I was just on a diet and as soon as I dropped the desired weight and got in better shape, I would ease up a little bit.

But my body rebelled. I was starving myself and working out too hard. One night while I was alone in my dorm, I ate everything I could get my hands on. Chips, toaster pastries, crackers, peanut butter, and chocolate were all devoured within minutes. Immediately shame, guilt, and regret poured over me. And since control had to be mine once again, I made myself throw up in a trash bag. I cinched the top and walked it out to the dumpster like it was something I did every day, like it was the same as the bag of wadded up tissues and crumpled paper that I had just taken out the day before. But it wasn't the same at all. Years of thoughts and actions had led to that moment, and once I climbed on the eating disorder train, it sped on too quickly for me to ever think about getting off again. I was stuck in an endless cycle of starving, binging, exercising, and starving some more. I no longer felt in control; I felt controlled. I soon got tired of going in circles. I got tired of feeling sick and exhausted and secluded. I really wanted to get better and I knew that the answer was probably found in reaching out for help. As I wrote in my journal, "confession will bring my behavior into the light. Do I want that? The darkness has been a very lonely place."

Not wanting to remain in my loneliness anymore, I confessed everything to my boyfriend (now husband). I felt that if I was going to be serious about our relationship, he needed to know what was happening. I couldn't talk to him face-to-face since we lived eight hours away from each other, so I wrote down and rehearsed everything I was going to say to him on the phone next time we talked. I quoted my lines and he responded with a plan.

"I think you'll do better if you come here. You'll be closer to your family. You'll be happier that we don't have to keep doing this long-distance relationship anymore. We can be together. I think it'll help." I agreed and made arrangements to transfer at the end of the semester. I started filling out paperwork to attend the university with him. Retrospectively, this is a point in which it would have been helpful for us to have reached out to someone who could have responded with more wisdom before either of us made a decision like this. Simply relocating in order to be closer to a long-distance boyfriend that I had been dating for less than a year ended up making things more difficult for me for the next three years. There are parts of David's suggestion that were completely true. I needed to be somewhere close to my best support system, which for me was my family. But they were still an hour and a half away, not close enough to be a daily part of my life. I transferred from a small school where I had developed meaningful godly relationships to a very large school where I only knew David. This decision had the unintentional consequence of actually diminishing my support system, and this should have been a vital thing to have considered before moving to a new place.

Before transferring, I started doing research. I wanted to know what I was facing and why it was happening to me. Most of all, I wanted to know how to stop. I looked up "how to stop dieting" and "when to be worried about eating behavior." What

I read startled me. I wasn't facing a bad habit or a diet gone wrong. I was dealing with a full-fledged psychological disorder, documented in big books and discussed by doctors and mental health professionals. On the one hand, that felt daunting and overwhelming, but on the other hand it helped me to understand that I wasn't just making this up. And it wasn't going to go away on its own. It was real and it was serious. I started to comprehend that help was beyond what David was able to handle, but I wasn't ready to confide in anyone else.

What Is an Eating Disorder?

The National Association of Anorexia Nervosa and Associated Disorders states that "every 62 minutes at least one person dies as a direct result of an eating disorder."[2] This association also states on their website that eating disorders have the highest mortality rate of any mental illness.[3] Eating disorders can lead to death. People with eating disorders are at a higher risk of dying by suicide,[4] and some eating disorders can lead to organ failure and severe infections. But knowing this grim information did not make me a changed person.

These statistics alone didn't motivate me to want to get better. They seemed so abstract and unimportant when compared with my ultimate desires to be thin. It was easy for me to pass off the information as something that could happen to someone else but not me . Since eating disorders involve disordered thoughts as well as behaviors, it is necessary to have helpers who can see the truth of the situation and help guide sufferers in the path of healing. Facts alone, however, are not going to change someone. Giving information on eating disorders will not make someone alter their perspective. No matter how terrible the consequences sound, it will never be enough to snap someone out of what they are doing. Researching an eating disorder is important for helpers, and sharing it can educate a sufferer on consequences that they may not have fully thought through, but don't expect education alone to change someone. A person cannot be changed merely on an intellectual level. There must be an ongoing, humble submission of the heart to God.

An eating disorder is defined by the DSM 5 as "a persistent disturbance of eating or eating-related behavior that results in the altered consumption or absorption of food and that significantly impairs physical health or psychosocial functioning."[5] It is a psychological disorder that is characterized by destructive eating habits. Those eating habits can range from restrictive eating to binge eating.

Three eating disorders tend to be the most common: anorexia nervosa, bulimia, and compulsive overeating (now identified as Binge Eating Disorder in the DSM).[6] If your experience doesn't conform to one of these specific types, don't allow that to distract you from continuing through this book. Many individuals do not possess all the "necessary" symptoms to be diagnosed with one of these disorders. The principles we discuss in this book will still be relevant for you. We will focus our attention on these three dominant types for the sake of clarity and brevity. A quick exploration of each type will be helpful.

Anorexia Nervosa

Anorexia nervosa refers to the habit of self-starvation which results in extreme weight loss. There is a morbid fear of weight gain which drives that self-starvation. The starvation and accompanying weight loss are accomplished through a combination of rigid dieting and excessive exercise (see appendix A for more on excessive exercise). Anorexia comes with a number of long-term serious consequences that are worth mentioning.

Bone Deficiencies. The lack of eating means that the bones do not get the calcium they need to remain strong. As a result, they are more prone to breaking, and osteoporosis can occur. The spinal column in particular deteriorates over time, which means that it can no longer support the body and keep it upright.

Skin Deficiencies. Malnutrition means that the skin isn't able to replenish itself and it becomes prone to bruising and general irritation. Individuals may note that their skin looks dry, rashy, and cracked.

Brain Deficiencies. Inadequate energy stores mean that the brain has less to draw from; it cannot produce cogent thoughts with ease and will instead find thought processing slower and more cumbersome.

Heart Deficiencies. Decreases in potassium in the body can create an irregular heartbeat, which can become fatal.

Other Symptoms. Imbalance in blood cell count, gastrointestinal imbalances, hypoglycemia, and (for women) a loss of menstrual period are additional complications that can develop.

These are serious symptoms which can be life-threatening if not corrected. Helpers need to know this so that they take seriously the dynamics at play and involve medical assistance immediately. Sufferers need to know this so that they face the reality of their condition. There are more annual deaths related to anorexia than any other mental illness.[7] It's that serious.

Bulimia

Bulimia is related to anorexia, but each has some distinct features. Bulimia refers to the consumption of large amounts of calories (called binging) and the elimination of those calories before digestion (called purging). The purging of calories can come in a couple of different forms: forced vomiting or overuse of laxatives. This disorder shares many of the same symptoms as anorexia, but it also has additional problems.

Intestinal Deficiencies. The overuse of laxatives means that the muscles in the intestines begin to decay. The body becomes dependent on the laxatives to assist in the elimination of food. When the laxatives aren't present in the body, severe constipation can result.

Hydration Deficiencies. Vomiting leads to dehydration, which leads the body to store up water in an effort to survive. Stored water, however, means that the face, abdomen, hands, legs, and feet may swell. This can become very confusing and distressing to someone with an eating disorder. Their habits are designed to cause them to lose weight, but their body, in an effort to survive, creates swelling. The sufferer, then, may be convinced that they are gaining weight and increase their efforts to lose weight.

Tissue Decay. The repeated exposure to acidity from vomiting can cause long-term damage to the teeth, esophagus, voice box, and stomach. The upper digestive system is not designed to handle repeated exposure to the acidity of vomit. In time, tooth enamel washes away, cavities occur, and eventually there can be complete tooth loss. This acidity can also cause damage to the esophagus and voice box. Furthermore, repeated vomiting depletes normal levels of stomach acid, which then prompts the stomach to produce more acid to replace what has been lost. Without any food in the stomach, the acid will eat away at the stomach wall and intestines, damaging the tissue and creating ulcers.

Binge Eating Disorder

This disorder is more than simply overeating, which we all do from time to time. The key idea here is a compulsive or emotionally unhealthy relation to eating. Instead of just the occasional feeling of being "stuffed," binging refers to overeating when not hungry or for reasons not related to hunger, feeling out of control around food, or eating without tasting or enjoying food. Like undereating, the overeating associated with binge eating can be damaging psychologically and physically. The consequences of binge eating disorder are more generally known, but they are worth listing: obesity, gastrointestinal imbalance, high cholesterol, heart disease, high blood pressure, stroke, diabetes, sleep apnea, and arthritis.

It may appear as though overeating is vastly different from undereating. There are obvious differences that make each unique, and yet there are some important similarities between the two types of disorders. Some research suggests that those who struggle with an eating disorder think about food for about 70 percent of their day.[8] They think about what they are going to eat, what they aren't going to eat, when they are going to eat, how to avoid eating, and what they will do after they eat. This is an obsession that can dominate a life. Furthermore, all three eating disorders use food or restriction of food as a means of meeting some desire, like comfort or control. The abuse of food is a manifestation of a deeper core issue. We will explore those common core issues later. Though the disorders are obviously different in presentation, many of the principles we discuss in this book will be relevant across the spectrum of eating disorders, and that is because each shares a lot in common with the others.

Eating Disorders and Addictions

There are a number of ways that eating disorders parallel addictive habits. Three parallels are worth mentioning.

First, both addictions and eating disorders involve behavior that can provide some measure of physical or mental pleasure or relief from stress. Individuals with eating disorders have described a sort of psychological high that accompanies the cycles of binging, purging, or starvation. This rush can come from the pleasurable intake of food, or the psychological sense of being in control, or the relief that occurs when we give into strong urges.

Secondly, both addictions and eating disorders become enslaving. Whatever pleasure or relief is derived from the characteristic behavior of the eating disorder, it is often followed by a sense of despair, guilt, and even physical pain. Many sufferers have a love/hate relationship with their eating disorder. They love it at times, and at other times want to quit. Many feel completely trapped in this cycle. What started out promising freedom becomes enslaving. Long after it feels good, those who develop an eating disorder find that they can't stop. This dynamic is very similar to the experience of those struggling with addiction.

Finally, both addictions and eating disorders can change us physiologically. We've seen this in our description of the symptoms of eating disorders above. It's important to note, however, that these physiological changes can make it very difficult to navigate toward recovery. When a destructive habit alters our physiology, our body can become stuck in the destructive pattern. Our bodies don't know how to relate to food properly. Like our mind, our bodies will need to be retrained to discern and appreciate hunger, fullness, pleasure, calmness, and health. These are all important considerations as you move forward.

These parallels are worth mentioning because we want to have realistic expectations about the process of change. As anyone who has struggled to quit smoking can attest, addictive habits do not always go away with ease, nor is the process of change as simple as deciding to make good choices. There is a lot involved in recovery, and it will be necessary to have patience with the process, patience with oneself, and an understanding of all that may be involved.

Interactive Exercise

The following exercise is designed to start a conversation about the particulars of the eating disorder that both the sufferer and the helper are attempting to address. Set aside a time when you can sit and discuss this section of the book. Pray together, and then share your answers to the following questions:

For the Sufferer

Review the symptoms listed above, and share with your helper what your experience has been. Which category of eating disorder do you most closely identify with? What is different, in your experience, from what has been described here? What symptoms are most concerning to you? How do you feel about the parallel between an eating disorder and addiction (can you relate; is it upsetting; does that parallel help you in any way)? How do you feel about yourself, your struggles, and God as you think through these things? What might it look like to imagine a life without these destructive eating habits?

For the Helper

Review the symptom lists for yourself. Which symptoms have you noticed in your companion? Which symptoms are most concerning to you? What have you learned about eating disorders from this chapter? What have you learned about yourself?

CHAPTER 2

Understanding Your Role and Embracing the Process of Change

In this chapter we are going to seek to clarify the role that both sufferers and helpers play in the process of change. Krista will share from her experience, explaining the role she played in her progress. She will describe the proper way to evaluate readiness for change and discuss the significance of opening up about your struggle as a first step. David will turn attention to the helper and describe the ways in which we must build trust and demonstrate love, giving tips on how to cultivate this in your dynamic. In each case it will be important to have realistic expectations about the process. God delights to bless the relationship between helpers and sufferers, but these relationships thrive best when each person's role is properly understood.

Reaching Out for Help

After feeling he had reached the limits of his ability to help me, David talked to our pastor.

"What did you tell him?" I snapped.

"I just told him what's going on. You haven't been eating. You've been lying to me. You refuse to talk to anyone else and I don't know how to help you. What was I supposed to do?"

"I don't know!" I shouted. "Not that! I didn't want anyone at church knowing about this. I can deal with it myself. I'm fine."

"Well, obviously you're not fine or we wouldn't be having this conversation. I'm trying to help you. You don't have to get angry with me."

"You should have asked me first." I started to leave the room.

"Don't put that on me," David answered. "I've asked you a million times to talk to someone and you keep saying you will. You said you were going to talk to your mom. You said you would call your friends from your old school. I can't do this by myself anymore!"

I felt betrayed and embarrassed. I had expected David to keep my secret even while my life was spinning out of control in front of him. I was ashamed that one more person saw my biggest flaw. I worried about what our pastor would think of me. I was angry, but I also felt relieved. I had been offered a chance to give up part of my burden. It was an invitation to finally start getting some help. After this incident I wrote in my journal:

> I know I wasn't safe while David kept silent about my issues . . . but I'm still so mad that he told. I'm scared that I will have to do something that will make me gain even more weight than I already have. I don't want people bugging me about this. I know I wasn't going to get any better if he had kept my problem to himself . . . I just don't really want to talk to him today. I don't even know if I want to get better. I wish I had never told him to begin with.

Though it didn't seem like it to me at the time, I know now that David was actually doing the most loving thing for me by sharing my struggle with our pastor. He risked losing our relationship in order to take me to safety. Sometimes love is risky like that. It involves making someone mad in order to get them the help that they need. Of course, as a general rule, helpers should allow sufferers to reveal their struggles and not speak too prematurely. Usually we recommend helpers first encourage sufferers to be the ones to share their struggle, but there does come a point at which safety must take priority. I had reached that point.

Just because David shared this information with someone in a position to help didn't automatically guarantee that I'd get better. I had to be willing to accept the help I was being offered—would I go on doing exactly what I had been doing, knowing that I could no longer keep it a secret, or would I release some of my control by allowing someone with more resources to start giving me help? The confession I had presented to my husband in the beginning of my struggle only gave me a weak version of accountability because he could not support that accountability with instruction. He knew enough to try to keep me from doing harmful things, but he didn't know what to tell me to do instead. He had given me multiple chances to reach out to people I thought would be helpful, but when I was getting worse and the situation started feeling dangerous, he made the decision to talk to our pastor, who, though not trained in eating disorders, was able to point us in the right direction. For us, the helper we chose was our pastor, but for others, it might be a school counselor or your primary care physician. Most people are not equipped with the information needed for lasting care of someone with an eating disorder, so it is important to reach out to someone who has the resources to point you in the right direction.

It Has to Become Your Own Request for Help

While it was beneficial for David to have reached out for help, I had to decide to take the next step for myself. A helper cannot force a sufferer into recovery by making choices for them. So that Sunday I stuck around after church. I looked our pastor in the face and said, "I'm ready to talk." I released some of my hold on the secret obsessions. I told him about my rituals that I performed behind closed doors. I told him about some of the thoughts I was having about my body and about needing control. I told him I was ready to change. Thankfully, I wasn't met with simplistic commands like "you need to do *this*," or "if you'd just do *that*." I was met with compassion. "I'm sorry you are going through this, Krista. I want to help you as much as I can." He gave us the names of medical professionals in our area, as well as the name of a Christian counselor who had been helpful to other members of our church.

My recovery was never a completely linear uphill process. If I were to make a graph of what my growth looked like, the line would have an overall upward climb but with individual jumps and dives along that path, creating spikes of highs and lows. Our pastor provided the first layer of help. Through regular meetings, our pastor promoted and encouraged honesty and accountability even when I didn't have good things to report. By always having David present in those sessions, there was a level to which it was harder for me to be deceitful about what had actually happened through the week. He also helped me to start looking at my eating disorder in light of how it affected my relationship with God. He used Scripture to point me to changes that I could make in my heart. The trained counselor that he referred me to provide the second layer of help. She started giving me practical steps to take. She had me report to her honestly about what my daily schedule looked like. It helped me to be more aware of how often I was thinking about food and how much time I was spending on my rituals. She helped me to set goals for each day and establish better routines.

After I reached out for help, I needed to understand my role as the recipient of help. I had to give up some of my privacy. I had to be okay with explaining where I had been and what I had been doing. I had to be okay with someone going with me to places I had usually gone by myself, such as the grocery store and the gym. And I had to be okay with more phone calls and more questions and more honesty. I also realized that I had closed myself off from all other relationships besides the one I had with David, and so I started pursuing people and allowing people back into my life. I went on shopping trips with ladies from church. I started having more phone conversations with our pastor's wife. I began to attend more church functions. Not everyone involved had to have the same amount of information about my struggle as those who were most closely helping me, but it was important to form a support system that could speak truth into my everyday life and help me when I was struggling. Our pastor offer biblical instruction and spiritual care, my counselor provided practical help, our pastor's wife gave me someone to call in immediate times of temptation and struggle, and various ladies from church provided love, encouragement, and friendship.

As much as I needed someone to come alongside me during this battle and as much as I valued the help that was being given to me, I could not expect anyone to keep me from harm 100 percent of the time. I also had to learn to be responsible with being alone. Yes, I needed someone on hand to ask me about my struggle and call me out when I was slipping into destructive patterns, but as my journey progressed, I also needed to be realistic about the role of a human helper. I could count on those around me for support and for extra protection. They could help talk me down when my thoughts were out of control. They could sit with me when I couldn't trust myself to be alone, but at the end of the day, they were not my guards, my babysitters, or my Holy Spirit. They could not completely cover over the ugly thoughts that caused my behavior to spiral. They could not cure the evil intentions that lurked deep in my heart. With the help of the Holy Spirit, I had to learn how to make daily choices to stop thinking the way I had been thinking. I had to turn from temptation when it came by calling a friend for help or by redirecting my behavior to a goal I had made for that day. I had to run toward the commands and encouragements that were placed before me in the Word of God by reading passages of Scripture and writing out three to five key truths and applications or by committing to doing a Bible study with a more mature woman from church. I had to resist the desires in my heart and cling to the only One who could change me by developing a better habit of daily prayer which oriented my heart to cry out to God first when I was in crisis. The gospel had already freed me from the enslaving power of sin, but I needed to daily believe that and live in light of it (Romans 6:6).

On one particular occasion I was sitting in my car outside of my empty house, feeling stressed and anxious, ready to perform my usual binging and purging routine. I called a couple people who were supporting my recovery process, none of whom answered. But instead of trying to stuff my anxiety down with food and purging, I began to pray.

I said, "God, I am really struggling. I don't want to do this. I want to feel better. I want to be free from this cycle. I want to be strong, but I'm really weak right now. Come and be strong for me. Help me to resist the temptation that is facing me right now." I continued to pray for hours. I had victory that night.

This was my life for the next few months: passionate, constant prayer, fighting temptation on a daily basis, choosing right when I really wanted to do wrong. But I had to *choose* to do this. I had to choose to pray. I had to choose to read my Bible. I had to choose not to go in the house where the cabinets were stuffed with fuel to feed my temptation. I had to decide not to buy the food or turn on the exercise video. Oftentimes I sat on the couch and read the book of Psalms until the feelings subsided. Even if I had to read the whole book and start over again, even if it took hours, I read until I could get up and move on with a new plan. I took walks and recited Scripture. I blasted praise music in the car. Instead of giving in to my urges, I began to saturate my mind and heart with the Word of God.

One big piece of the equation was facing my thought life. I saw many counselors over the years, many of which gave me homework that promoted a positive self-image and positive life strategies. As time went by, however, I saw that these tactics were not helping me to get better and were often making me frustrated. The positive self-talk did not acknowledge that I struggled with sin. Yes, I needed to stop the cycle of self-loathing, but that was going to come by focusing on Jesus and not myself. I could take great comfort in what he had done for me and the power I had to live with new patterns because of his grace.

With this is mind, I had to daily take my thoughts captive to obey Christ (2 Corinthians 10:5), which meant I had to train myself to recognize when I was thinking loathsome, destructive thoughts about myself. But I couldn't just take the thoughts away; I had to replace them with truth. Philippians 4:8 became my filter for where to set my mind: whatever was true, honorable, just, pure, commendable, or worthy of praise. My feelings wanted me to believe the lie that nobody loved me. The truth, whether or not my emotions agreed, was that God loved me more than I could imagine. My feelings wanted me to believe that how I felt about my body was what defined my worth. The truth, however, was that I was fearfully and wonderfully made (Psalm 139:14).

The process of retraining my thoughts was a daily choice that took years to build into a habit, but only part of this process was dependent on me. I had to realize that I had an even stronger power within me. Not a power of self-motivation but of the Holy Spirit. Instead of the self-motivational speeches some of my counselors encouraged me to adopt, I had to learn the practice of relying on the grace of God to overcome my weaknesses and to experience freedom (2 Corinthians 3:17; 12:9).

I don't want you to think that everything I just described meant I was free of my struggle with food. Far from it. There was so much more that God had to (and did) teach me. There was (and is) so much more to learn, but these foundational truths of being transparent to those close to me, seeking God's help through the help of others, learning to pray, and learning to fill my mind with Scripture were the basis for moving forward by faith.

Readiness for Change

In the beginning, I asked for help out of desperation. I felt out of control. I didn't feel like myself anymore. I didn't like that my life felt like it was careening towards a cliff all the time. I also had a great awareness of what I had lost. In my life before an eating disorder, I had been social and active. Relationships had always made me nervous, but at least I use to have them. I was part of a group of friends. I played on sports teams, participated in church youth group, and was involved in various student clubs at school. But in my life with an eating disorder, I was stuck in my apartment all the time counting calories and doing workout videos. I didn't eat out. I didn't go to parties. I felt too tired to go to sporting events. My life was on autopilot. I avoided investing into relationships so that I could focus on keeping track of calories and exercising. I finally agreed to reach out for help because I wanted all of that to change. I wanted my life to look different.

I would like to say I was motivated to change by a deep grief over my sin against God. I would like to say I wanted to change because I knew God wanted better for me or because I loved God so much that I wanted to obey him. Those were not my initial reasons for pursuing change. I just wanted my old life back, and I was tired of feeling so awful all the time. Likewise, if you suffer from an eating disorder, you may also feel that your reasons for change aren't all that commendable, but I want to encourage you that God may use a lesser motivation in order to bring you around to where you need to be. If you are waiting for such a strong desire to honor God that you immediately surrender your eating disorder to him, you may never make progress. I wanted freedom from my eating disorder, and so I was open to change. This was an important starting place that propelled me in the right direction, and this can be an important starting place for you as well.

Taking responsibility for your part in an eating disorder will involve seeing both the sin and the suffering interwoven in your eating disorder. It involves confessing your struggle to someone who can help, such as a parent, teacher, pastor, or counselor, and committing to accountability. It involves diligent prayer to allow God to show you the deeply-rooted motivations that are the source of your behavior. And lastly it involves fighting to change your desires, thoughts, and attitudes by applying Scripture. If you are reading this book with someone else, then you have already confessed your struggle to someone. Over the remainder of this book you will have opportunity to address your desires, thoughts, and attitudes as well. At this moment, however, it is important to contemplate your readiness to change. This was my critical first step as well.

The following descriptors outline a spectrum of readiness that highlights the various stages you might traverse in coming to a point of decision. Examine this list with your helper and identify where you land on the spectrum.

Denial. At this stage I do not think I have a persistent problem. While I may notice some negative behavior from time to time, I honestly believe that I am still in control and can manage my world.

Considering. At this stage I am beginning to recognize that some of my habits or rituals might be problematic. While I am not making any changes just yet, I am considering the possibility of change and what it might require of me.

Investigating. At this stage I know I have a problem and need to change, but I am not quite prepared to do anything. I am willing to begin researching, exploring, and looking into what change will require. I am scared to let go of my habits, and so I want to know what to expect before I make a commitment.

Seeking. At this stage I am willing to change but I am scared and not sure if I can do it. I am seeking guidance and help from someone who will help me make those first steps toward confession and recovery.

Ready. Finally, at this stage, I am not just willing to change, I really want it. I am willing to do whatever it takes to be rid of my eating disorder. I am not naive about the cost, and I know that some days I may still want my disordered habits, but I am ready to fight through even those feelings. I have a friend to help me, and I am beginning to make steps towards change.

Where would you rate yourself today? Revisit this spectrum from time to time as you make progress and evaluate yourself afresh.

The Helper's Role

"I just want my wife back." I (David) was frustrated and feeling helpless. What could I do? What did Krista need? Why couldn't she just stop these behaviors? If I could have changed this struggle for her, I would have.

In the early years of our marriage, I did not know much about counseling, and I knew nothing about eating disorders. My own immaturity often made my response to Krista's struggle primarily about disruption to my life and my dreams. For a long while I tried to avoid the topic, hoping it would just get better or that she would "grow out of it." As we progressed, I thought that I needed to be tough with her. I thought she was simply living in sin and needed to repent. So, I was sometimes demanding and even harsh in my approach. This practice not only completely bypassed the suffering component of eating disorders, but also failed to model Christ's gentle approach to coming alongside the broken.

What is a loving and effective way to support and encourage a loved one in the process of change? Knowing the difference between forcing change and cultivating it can go a long way in helping to provide care. Often helpers are so desperate for their loved ones to recover that they will try to force change. We use intervention, manipulation, confrontation, control, and consequence in an effort to force them to make better choices. Such "tools" may have short-term gains, but they are unsuccessful in the long run. Addiction specialist Carlo DiClemente has keenly observed this truth. He writes:

There are many examples of how external pressures or control (even positive incentives like money or privileges) often produce short-term but not lasting addictive behavior change unless the individual is ready to cooperate. . . . Individuals jailed for drug-use offenses, even for significant periods of time, often return to use upon release. Mandated treatments produce mixed results. . . . Curtailing supplies often creates greater demand and vigorous black markets. Clearly, external pressure is not the magic that necessarily or automatically motivates consideration of change.[9]

There is no silver bullet that helpers can use to produce change in their loved one. Change has to be internally motivated. The sufferer must determine to apply themselves to the hard work of restructuring their life. No one else can make this decision for them.

This is frustrating for helpers. It certainly was frustrating for me. I would often resort to ultimatums and pressure to get Krista to make changes. I remember threatening divorce at least once in the process. The way I responded was sinful and wrong, but it also represented something of the helplessness I felt in the face of this ongoing problem. I couldn't force her to change, and my pressure didn't help. The solution for the helper, however, is not to do nothing. We have a responsibility to help. Instead of ultimatums and attempts to force repentance, cultivating change in others involves building trust and demonstrating love. People need support in order to change. This is why Paul says that we need to "bear one another's burdens" (Galatians 6:2). If our loved ones trust us and know that we love them, our offer to bear burdens is more likely to be believed as genuine and received well. Without trust and love, offers to help will feel like attempts to control.

Building Trust and Loving Well

Counselor Diane Langberg states that building trust and loving well requires three things: talking, tears, and time.[10] Each component plays a part in cultivating rapport with our loved ones. Don't assume that just because of your relational status that you automatically have a loved one's trust. When it comes to sin, addictive habits, and sorrows, our insecurities plague all of us. In fact, those we are closest to are sometimes those with whom we are least willing to share these parts of our life. We may often fear disappointing those closest to us. Or we can sense that those who are closest to us are the least likely to be understanding. The deep intimacy in a relationship creates strong emotions, and helpers can overreact, panic, and be especially intense when we fear for our loved one's safety. Building trust, then, regardless of the longevity and depth of your relationship, will be required.

Cultivating trust begins with dialogue. Conversation is partly what this book is designed to help stimulate. I regret not being more willing to enter into deeper discussion with Krista in the beginning. I was unsettled by her habits. They were behaviors and anxieties that I simply couldn't relate to and had trouble understanding. Why, for example, was going to a restaurant so upsetting to Krista? It didn't make sense to me, and the strength of her reaction to the idea of eating out was confusing. In many ways, my hesitance to discuss things with her was driven by fear. What if she told me something that I wasn't prepared to hear? What if she told me something that was more serious than I could handle? What if I found out something and didn't know how to respond? These fears were selfish. They were driven by my own comfort and security and self-perceived competency. Perfect love, however, casts out fear (1 John 4:18). Loving my wife meant that I needed to talk to her about her problems. Loving those in your life who suffer from an eating disorder will mean encouraging them to talk about it.

You will initially facilitate this dialogue by asking lots of questions. To be truly helpful, we must do our best to understand. Ask questions about your loved one's personal experiences, thoughts, anxieties, and desires. Listen carefully. Pay attention to what is said and not said. Note the body language, tone of voice, and sense of despair in their communication.

The next part of loving well involves regularly reaching out. Demonstrate concern by checking in on how they are doing. Eating disorders are isolating habits. They thrive in the darkness, and those who engage in disordered eating feel a sense of shame and embarrassment that keeps them from pulling others into their world. By engaging with your loved one, you are inviting them out into the light, you are showing them that you care, and you are reminding them that you are available to listen. They don't have to suffer alone.

Helpful dialogue does not always involve giving advice. Any help that begins with the words, "You just need to . . ." is usually simplistic and unhelpful. Furthermore, people don't want to talk with those who are going to constantly lecture, preach, or prescribe. They want friends who will listen well before speaking. Confrontation must never be our first response. The Bible encourages us to share in the pain of those we love. Paul, writing to the Romans, instructs, "Rejoice with those who rejoice, weep with those who weep" (Romans 12:15). This is what it looks like to genuinely and intimately care for one another. In the case of caring for loved ones with eating disorders, it may be that we actually cry with them, especially as they share the painful stories behind their disordered habits.

It is tempting to conclude that because eating disorders may involve sinful choices and destructive habits, helpers should focus first and foremost on calls to repentance. Yet we need to remember how hard change is, how painful sin is, and how complex motives are. Yes, our loved ones will need to repent, but their sin (or perhaps the sins of another) has still caused them heartache and trouble. If we can only see their sin and not their sorrow, then we will not really see them, and we will not really be helpful. Jesus, even as he acknowledges the wickedness of Jerusalem, the city that stones the prophets, nevertheless longs to comfort her children (Luke 13:34). Be compassionate in your help. Sit with friends who are sorrowful, listen, cry with them, and acknowledge the hardship of what they are experiencing. As you grow in compassion, you will also sense the need to move with them slowly. Developing trust takes time.

Providing Long-Term Support

Most of us don't mind waiting a little while with those who are suffering, but eventually we expect that their problem will go away and the person will get on with their life. We tend to lose patience when suffering is prolonged. Your loved one's eating disorder is not going to dissipate quickly. They will need to know that you're committed for the long haul. The more consistent and faithful you are in your care, the more they will sense that you truly do care about them.

No one, of course, is perfect at long-term support and patience. There will be days when it is harder for you to sit and listen, harder for you to be understanding and compassionate. The longer the recovery process takes, the more susceptible you will become to impatience and what is called *compassion fatigue.* Compassion fatigue is the burnout and exhaustion felt by someone who has become consumed by the frequency or intensity of caring for another. It describes the prolonged weariness that we feel when we spend a lot of our time and energy caring for another. It's important, then, that we take good care of ourselves too, with plenty of sleep, meaningful relaxation, and seeking supportive relationships of our own for sharing our burdens.[11]

It's also important that we confess our failures and ask for forgiveness from our loved ones when we fail them. When I was short or impatient with Krista, or when I was cold or annoyed, I needed to confess it and ask her forgiveness. We grow in wisdom and grace and demonstrate love by admitting our failures and seeking forgiveness.

Not Forcing Change

Change must be an internal decision on the part of those enslaved to eating disorders. Helpers cannot force repentance or change for those that they love. Yet, this does not leave us completely helpless. Change happens best within the context of meaningful relationships and consistent support. As a helper, you are in a position to cultivate a desire for change. Through talking, tears, and time, you demonstrate that you are committed to those who are suffering, that you will walk with them, and that you see them for who they are. You will be there to grieve setbacks, to celebrate victories, and to encourage endurance. Your role is a necessary one, even if you cannot be the one to bring lasting transformation.

Interactive Exercise

In the spirit of building trust, the following conversation is designed to encourage sharing and listening to some of the more difficult aspects of a sufferer's experience of their eating disorder. Answer the following questions and plan a time to discuss them with one another.

For the Sufferer

What is one of the most difficult aspects of your eating disorder? What do you most fear about it? What do you most fear about sharing this struggle with someone else? What is one thing that your helper has done for you that you appreciate? What is one thing you would not want your helper to do? Based on the scale provided in this chapter, how would you rate your readiness to change? What did you learn about yourself from reading this chapter?

For the Helper

The following is a listening evaluation. Fill it out and consider the strengths and weaknesses of your listening skills. Ask your loved one to also evaluate your listening skills so you can discover any blind spots. What is one listening skill that you can work to improve? How can you take steps to change? What is one thing that your loved one shared with you that surprised you? What is something about your loved one that you appreciate? What is one thing that you learned about yourself from reading this chapter?

In the following evaluation[12] circle the answers that best describe you (Almost Never, Sometimes, Not Sure, Usually, Almost Always).

1. I find it easy to listen to others.

O———O———O———O———O

ALMOST NEVER   SOMETIMES   NOT SURE   USUALLY   ALMOST ALWAYS

2. Others can tell that I am interested in what they have to say.

O———O———O———O———O

ALMOST NEVER   SOMETIMES   NOT SURE   USUALLY   ALMOST ALWAYS

3. I can accurately represent others' thoughts and feelings back to them.

O———O———O———O———O

ALMOST NEVER   SOMETIMES   NOT SURE   USUALLY   ALMOST ALWAYS

4. When I listen, I seek to understand, not simply waiting my turn to speak.

O———O———O———O———O

ALMOST NEVER   SOMETIMES   NOT SURE   USUALLY   ALMOST ALWAYS

5. I do not interrupt others when they talk.

ALMOST NEVER SOMETIMES   NOT SURE   USUALLY ALMOST ALWAYS

6. I ask questions to draw out more from the person speaking.

ALMOST NEVER SOMETIMES   NOT SURE   USUALLY ALMOST ALWAYS

7. I don't rush conversations in order to end them.

ALMOST NEVER SOMETIMES   NOT SURE   USUALLY ALMOST ALWAYS

8. Others feel that I can be trusted with their thoughts and emotions.

ALMOST NEVER SOMETIMES   NOT SURE   USUALLY ALMOST ALWAYS

9. When I respond, I build on what the other person shared.

ALMOST NEVER SOMETIMES   NOT SURE   USUALLY ALMOST ALWAYS

10. I can be patient in conversations even when I am tired.

ALMOST NEVER SOMETIMES   NOT SURE   USUALLY ALMOST ALWAYS

CHAPTER 3

Understanding Our Motives

People develop eating disorders for a variety of reasons, and no single cause satisfactorily explains the origin of every person's disordered eating habits. We can point to experiences of developmental trauma, genetics, and cultural pressures as contributing factors, yet none of these elements can be held solely responsible. Each person, the Bible tells us, is lured into sin by their own desire (James 1:14). The heart is the engine of human behavior. We do what we do, because we want what we want.[13] In this chapter you are going to learn about some of the common motives that lay at the root of an eating disorder. You are going to hear Krista's firsthand experience of identifying her heart motives, and you will learn to do your own self-evaluation. Helpers will learn to assist in this process by looking for key themes and asking the right questions. In order to stop disordered eating behaviors, we must first learn to confront our desires.

Krista's Story

Two years had passed since I first started experiencing symptoms of an eating disorder. I had done everything I knew to do in order to get better, but I was still struggling. Though I learned a lot and had experienced some growth, there were moments that felt like nothing had changed. I wouldn't be as diligent to apply what I knew to do or I would do what I thought I was supposed to be doing and nothing would happen as a direct correlation so

I would get frustrated and give up for a period of time. I would pray and I wasn't immediately delivered in that exact moment so I dismissed anything God was doing as insignificant because it wasn't obvious, quick and instantaneous. Instead of experiencing consistent growth, I felt at best stagnant and at worst slightly backslidden. I was no longer feeling hopeful that I would someday get better. If God wasn't going to completely heal me on my timetable, then I was out. But recovery doesn't work that way. Sanctification doesn't work that way. It's not a sprint to the finish. It's a long, steady trod. Deep, desperate prayer can be a means by which God brings healing but only because through it your heart is being inclined more to him. As a quick-fix gimmick, prayer had failed me. As a consistent, obedient bowing of my heart to God it would eventually draw me back to him. But the frustration of working so hard and not seeing the desired results was enough to send me into somewhat of a spiritual crisis.

I stood in my kitchen, knowing that a binge was coming and both wanting and not wanting it. Something inside of me insisted that I had to take part in the whole ritual, from start to finish or everything I had tried to accomplish through calorie counting and restricting would be lost. Performing all that my eating disorder told me to do felt empowering but also horribly shameful. I longed for what it promised me—control, acceptance, affirmation and achievement—yet my heart constantly cried out for an alternative. I wanted reassurance that God loved me, but I still was struggling to be honest with him about this part of my life. Amidst trying to determine if God cared about my actions or not, I had a thought that was so clear that I almost spoke it: *God, I feel like you are telling me not to do this, but I don't care anymore. I'm tired of doing what you ask me to do and getting nothing out of it. Other people are telling me that trusting you will get me through this, but that is not my experience right now. I feel like you are failing me. I'd rather just go back to what I was doing and at least get something that I want.*

In that moment, I lost sight of the reason for true obedience. Instead of doing what is right in order to show love and honor to the creator and sustainer of my life, I wanted my actions to save me somehow. Though obedience does have benefits for me, good experiences are just the side effect and should not be the only desired end. The goal of obedience is always glory to God, not glory to me. Because I wanted tangible benefits, thinness— feeling the control and success of seeing pounds melt away—was more important to me than trusting God and being obedient to him. So, I turned back to the trenches of my eating disorder and I remained there for a few years. I continued to go to church and make a pretense of obedience, but I often didn't want to face a God I knew I was consistently and intentionally disobeying in order to get what I wanted. But despite my desire to hide my actions from him, he made it clear to me that he had never let me go. Through the circumstances and people he placed in my life, he eventually persuaded me that he could be trusted and that he truly had my good in mind.

While at home visiting my parents, I went to their church. Many of the same people still attended there from when I was a kid, including Emily, my sister's best friend. She had always been like an older sister to me. We fought like sisters, and we cared for each other like sisters. Her advice was often enough to keep me out of whatever trouble I was about to get myself into. I could trust her to be straightforward with me, and I had matured enough not to want to punch her in the face when she told me what I needed to hear. I looked up to her because of her spiritual strength, her knowledge of the Bible, and her desire to follow God. I felt that she was a safe person to share my struggles with and that she would be helpful to point me in the right direction.

"I have something I need to talk to you about," I told her, in a barely audible whisper at the end of a service. I looked around to make sure no one else was listening.

: could sense my reluctance to share in such close proximity to other people. "Why don't you come over to my place?" she suggested.

Her house was small, and books were shelved in every corner. We thumbed through them, and it was quiet for a while before I finally spoke up. "So . . . I don't really know how to put this, but I have been struggling a lot lately with eating issues. Well, I guess it's more than that. I . . . I . . . have an eating disorder. I've tried to get help, but I don't know what I'm supposed to do."

We talked for a while. Emily asked me a lot of questions. And then our conversation led us back to the bookshelves. She scanned the titles and then pulled out a book called *Idols of the Heart* by Elyse Fitzpatrick. It was worn around the edges and the cover was bent. "I can't say that I know what you are going through," she said. "But I read this book, and I think it will help."

I remember feeling a little disappointed. I was expecting a spiritual epiphany that would rush over me and wash all my eating problems away. I was expecting a personal sermon that would change my heart and heal me entirely. But instead I got a book. I wanted to be better. I wanted her to fix me. I didn't want to read a book. But, eventually, I did read it. I read about how idols aren't just carved images. They are our "thoughts, desires, longings and expectations that we worship in the place of the true God."[14] I studied, not just Elyse's words, but the notes that Emily had written in the margins. *Am I trusting God with his plans, or am I looking for something that I personally can control?* I was crushed under the statement, "If you are willing to sin to obtain your goal or if you sin when you don't get what you want, then your desire has taken God's place and you're functioning as an idolater."[15] The reason I felt guilty, the reason I felt sneaky and awful and in darkness, was because I wasn't just trying to obtain something that I couldn't reach. It was because I was trying to replace God with something else.

I then started to realize the true motives behind what I was doing. I was still hoping that mastery of my body would save me from what I imagined to be a bottomless ravine of self-doubt and insecurity. The feelings of achievement, success, and acceptance in general were and always had been my gods. Those ideas weren't focused on any one thing most of the time, which made them abstract and impossible to obtain. My eating disorder had just become a means by which to achieve those goals. Achieving my goal weight represented a means to control my destiny, be an approvable size, and be safe from criticism (my own or others'). I was terrified of what it might look like to lay down these idols. I didn't know how I might spiral without constantly grasping at rituals to keep me safe. An eating disorder gave me something to fall back on when I felt that something in my life was beyond my ability to control. I didn't know what it would be like not to have the sense of comfort I got through binging and purging. Without calories to calculate, I couldn't imagine anything else that would make me feel secure.

As I read the words on the pages of Fitzpatrick's book, combined with the words of Scripture, I began to have a clearer picture of what I was dealing with. I learned that an eating disorder brings disruption, chaos, and destruction, while living according to the design of my Creator would bring satisfaction, peace, and a blessed life. I learned that I didn't have to fight alone because God had sent the Holy Spirit to help me turn from my destructive behaviors and turn toward God and his truth. I learned that God and his love can truly be enough for me. I began to question the things that I had hoped would bring me joy. I didn't walk away from the book healed, or even close to it, but I did walk away with a clearer picture of what was in my heart and what I was truly facing. By recognizing a part of my behavior as it truly was—sin—I was ready to set up a better plan for fighting against it. I had spent years thinking that I could simply restructure my life with new schedules and mantras and step-by-step plans, all of which focused primarily on behavior and only made me trust in myself more. On their own these things produced failure. It was exposing and humiliating to admit my shortcomings, but by doing so I was able to root out the ugliness I had built up in my heart and begin to replace it with the purity of conformance to God's Word. And it was better for me to see my actions as sin, because sin has a remedy—the life, death and resurrection of Jesus. The gospel is a complete redemptive rescue mission that could only be fully carried out if I was willing to accept that I was in need of being rescued.

Common Motives Underlying Eating Disorders

We might be tempted to think that eating disorders are all about food. That makes sense, but disordered food habits are really symptoms of deeper issues. In order to really find freedom, we must learn to look deeper, to go beneath the surface of a binge, purge, or restrictive dietary plan. We must examine the heart. There are several common themes that accompany eating disorders. Whatever the specifics of the particular struggles of your situation, it is likely that you will be able to relate to one or more of these themes.

Control

This is a dominant motivation behind many eating disorders. Even as we explore other themes, we will see that control often works in tandem with other factors. Destructive food habits are often an effort to exercise control in a specific area of life as a response to feeling vulnerable in another area of life. Krista, for example, used food to help her feel more secure when she realized that she could not control how other people viewed her, or how her life was going to turn out. This motive is particularly evident in restrictive habits, where denying bodily hunger and appetite is the mind's attempt to achieve independence from the body. It is an effort to say, "I am in control of myself; my impulses and urges must submit to me." The control can be overt, or it can manifest in more subtle forms. Destructive habits can pursue control in one of three ways:

1. **Mastery.** Sometimes people use restrictive food habits or compulsive exercise in order to fulfill the desire to have power over their bodies or urges. The goal in such instances is to demonstrate a strong and independent willpower.

2. **Protection.** Some people may use compulsive eating in order to keep others at bay, to make themselves "unattractive," or to be invisible to unwanted attention. They may think, *If I am "fat" no one will want me, and if no one wants me, then no one can hurt me.*

3. **Compensation.** Still others might use food or disordered eating to compensate for other weaknesses. This sort of mentality says, "If I can't be good at ___, then I will be good at restricting my food."

In each case, control is an underlying issue. Sufferers seek to provide themselves a measure of comfort from the unpredictable and uncontrollable world around them. Efforts at control are often rooted in fear. They may attempt to control things because they are afraid of being vulnerable and because manipulation and control offer some hope of safety. To hearts assaulted in this way, eating disorders offer a temporary but ultimately false sense of security. "Cast your anxieties on food," or "Cast your anxieties on self-discipline" become cheap but alluring alternatives to Jesus's invitation to "[cast] your anxieties on him because he cares for you" (1 Peter 5:7). Whenever our hearts look elsewhere for the comfort that only God's presence can give, we will always lack the true support and stability we need.

Self-Medication

Food and/or destructive eating habits can be a means of self-medicating against negative emotions. Those who carry fears, whether of other people or of circumstances, who feel betrayed or rejected, or who suffer from traumatic memories or any other strongly negative emotions might use food, restriction, or exercise to make themselves feel better. Such behaviors can become a means of comfort, a respite from anxiety, and a general mood regulator. Such emotional dynamics are serious issues that must be addressed before people can find lasting change in their habits.

Appearance

Our society tells us that thin is good, and thick is bad. Many have bought into this lie and are convinced that they must be thin. Some buy into this ideal with such intensity and have such a morbid fear of gaining weight that no amount of thinness is enough. A popular phrase captures this idea: nothing tastes as good as skinny feels. That's the mindset of many who, even if they reach a "target weight" (which is often set dangerously low) still aren't satisfied.

God, however, does not value thinness. Elyse Fitzpatrick, who suffered with an eating disorder, notably said, "You know, I've read the Bible straight through many times, and I've never found any Scripture that commands or even commends thinness!"[16]

God is interested in our heart. He looks not on the outward appearance but at the inner person (1 Samuel 16:7; 2 Corinthians 5:12). Consider what Proverbs 31:30 (NIV) says, "Charm is deceptive, and beauty is fleeting; but a woman who fears the LORD is to be praised."

Physical beauty is fleeting; it doesn't last. The way you appear now will change over the course of your life. But the man or woman who "fears the Lord" has something truly worthy of praise. Godly character lasts and has real value. It's of far greater value than external glamour. This truth, like many essential matters of Christian faith, is much easier to give verbal consent to than it is to internalize. But what would it look like to really believe, deep down, that despite the constant insistence of the world around us, what really matters about us is the beauty of our hearts?

Pride

It may seem strange to think of pride as a common motive driving an eating disorder. Many of the men and women who struggle with destructive eating habits will tell you that they are incredibly insecure. That was definitely true in Krista's case. The reality, however, is that even behind those insecurities can be a great deal of pride.

Often there is pride that develops with regard to the specific eating habits. This is particularly common among those with restrictive habits. There is a sense of pride in being able to deny hunger impulses, to control eating, and to lose weight. This pride thrives on comparison. Someone struggling with anorexia may look at those who can't control their eating and in turn take a great deal of conceit in that comparison, silently and subtly assuring themselves, *I am stronger than them.* This contorted confidence develops because of the degree of willpower they seem to have. This pride of course doesn't last long, however for comparisons always betray. There's always someone thinner, stronger, prettier, fitter, better looking, happier—and on it goes.

Connected with pride may be the related issue of self-righteousness. Some people with an eating disorder may think, *I am better, more righteous, because of the way I eat or the way I restrict or the fact that I purge.* Or, *I keep my food rules; I don't gain weight.*

But what makes us righteous? Only Christ! Neither eating nor restricting, neither purging nor binging makes us holy and acceptable to God. Only Jesus's willing, gracious offering of himself for us sinners can cleanse us and give us the deep sense of inner righteousness that we long for.

Punishment

The final motivator follows closely on the heels of the previous. In this category, a person uses eating behaviors as a means of atonement for sin. A person might subconsciously punish themselves by restricting food, binging on food, or utilizing some other destructive habit. The logic might look like this:

- I've been bad, so I am not allowed to eat.
- I've been bad, so I must punish myself by binging.

Ultimately, such attempts at atonement lead us away from true atonement. In seeking to cleanse ourselves of sins (whether real or perceived), we look away from Christ's atoning work on the cross. The Bible tells us that no one is justified by works (Galatians 2:16). Only Jesus's perfect sacrifice cleanses us from sin! We must look to him alone.

It is important to note that when it comes to identifying our motives, we are not simply interested in identifying our unhealthy behaviors. Ultimately, we want to understand how our particular destructive habits express the deeper motivations of our hearts. How does your eating disorder function *down deep?* What "job" is it doing? Does restricting help you feel in control? Does the experience of binging and purging help you drown out feelings of shame or pain? Is overeating a way to punish yourself for sins you can't bear to think about? Such questions may not be quickly answered; they require patience to discern. Let's consider how we can discern the specific motives in our hearts.

Discerning Your Motives

Perhaps one of those common motives mentioned above immediately resonates with your situation. For many, however, discerning your heart motivations can be a complicated task. It's complicated because it isn't always easy to know our hearts well. Jeremiah tells us that the heart is desperately wicked and deceitful; he asks, "[W]ho can understand it?" (Jeremiah 17:9). Apart from God's help, we can never understand our deepest motives. Discernment is also complicated because our motivations change over time. What motivated you in the beginning—perhaps weight loss—can morph over time to become something quite different, like pride. It will take some careful attention and patience to draw out the motivations of our hearts.

You can begin to understand your motivations by exploring your thought patterns. Paul says that transformation happens through the renewal of the mind (Romans 12:2). As you strive to grow and change, you will need to confront any false thought patterns that have ensnared you in destructive behaviors. There are a few behaviors and thought patterns that those struggling with an eating disorder often need to confront.

Food Rules

Those who suffer from an eating disorder often have certain "food rules"—self-imposed standards, whether formalized or subconscious, which guide a person's interaction with food (e.g., no eating after 8:00 p.m., no dessert unless you earn it, you must purge if you eat fattening foods, etc.). Sometimes people know immediately what their "food rules" are, and sometimes they need to think about it. It may be that certain "rules" operate subconsciously, dictating their orders from the shadows. This is one reason it can be useful to write out your disordered habits together with their self-imposed rules. Helpers should encourage their loved ones to share these lists for the sake of conversation and accountability. Sin and death thrive on darkness and secrecy, but those who want to be healed come into the light (1 John 1:5–10).

Your particular food rules reveal what you are thinking at a deeper level. They are related to other concepts like shame, fear, and control. Thinking about your particular food rules and trying to connect them to your motives can be a productive exercise. Helpers might ask questions about specific food rules and discuss possible connections between that rule and various motivations. As you look for patterns among your self-imposed rules and consider what these rules have in common, helpers should listen with deep humility, gentleness, and prayerful patience. The following questions can guide both individual reflection and conversations between sufferer and helper.

- What are your food rules?
- What do these food rules have in common with one another?
- How long have you been using each specific food rule?
- How have your food rules evolved over time?

Extremes

Many people struggle with thinking in extremes. In this mental state there is no room for grey; no middle ground. Everything is either black or white, all or nothing. Either you are the best, or you are nothing. People are either all good or all bad. Life lived in this frame of mind often tends towards the negative and self-defeating, with a tendency to dismiss any positive event or circumstance. In addition, negative thought patterns tend to grow, progressing towards worst-case scenarios. Not getting a date turns into, "I am going to be alone the rest of my life." Not getting a desired compliment turns into, "People think I am ugly." Fear of eating turns into, "I will never be able to be happy eating (or never able to stop eating)." Eating a cookie turns into, "I am going to gain ten pounds by tomorrow." Extreme thinking often appears illogical to outsiders, but its powerful emotional effects are very real.

As sufferers and helpers identify examples of extreme thoughts, they will be able to see more clearly the large motives at work. Helpers can serve their loved ones by graciously pointing out instances of extreme thinking or when they see a sufferer bent toward an excessively negative outlook. Identifying such thought patterns is one step toward revealing the underlying motivations of our thoughts. The task of wisdom, as Scripture counsels us, involves drawing out the reasons of the heart that are hidden in the "deep waters" within us (Proverbs 20:5).

- What are some examples of "extreme" thinking that you engage in? (Helpers may be able to offer some input here.)

- When are you most tempted towards these types of thoughts?
- Do you notice any patterns or common themes in your extreme thoughts?

Triggers

The temptation to practice a disordered habit can occur at any moment in the day, but the impulse is usually triggered by something specific—an event or situation that redirects the attention and emotions towards the disordered behavior (i.e., binging, purging, compulsive exercising, etc.).

Triggers are as diverse as the people who experience them. For some, stepping onto the scale may trigger a temptation to overindulge in exercise. For others it might be seeing the pair of jeans that they keep in the closet, the pair that don't fit but which are there to remind them not to eat. For others, feelings of stress or guilt trigger destructive behaviors. Cataloging when and how you or your loved one experiences disordered thoughts or behaviors can help to identify these triggers. As you learn to identify the situational triggers that prompt disordered behavior, you may be in a better position to draw conclusions about the motives at play and, as you work toward recovery, to know what situations, thoughts, or activities might need to be avoided or treated with special care.

- What triggers you to indulge in disordered eating behaviors?
- When are you most frequently triggered?

Hunger and Fullness

Eating disorders often cloud an understanding of hunger and fullness. The distortion of these feelings leads people to make unhealthy associations. If you eat when you are sad, then you may begin to confuse the feeling of hunger with the experience of sadness. As a result, despite having nothing to be sad about in the moment, a natural feeling of hunger may actually cause you to feel sad. And, of course, feeling sad may instinctively trigger a sense of hunger. The number of associations is limitless, but perhaps you can relate to some of these:

- Hunger produces anxiety. (I feel like I am not in control, or I might lose control.)
- Hunger feels good. (I feel like I am losing weight.)
- Resisting hunger builds pride. (I feel like I can control this.)
- Eating when hungry leads to failure or shame. (I feel like I wasn't strong enough.)
- Hunger prompts regret. (I feel like I am going to eat too much.)

Likewise, fullness can be confused with negative emotions. Feeling full may be associated with feelings of shame, failure, weakness, or lack of self-control. Hunger and fullness are, of course, normal and healthy experiences, given by God as part of his good creation. But those suffering from an eating disorder will need to become reattuned to the natural rhythms of their bodily sensations. Identifying what negative emotional associations we currently experience around food, purging, or restriction will help us to better understand the needs, longings, and dynamics of our hearts and, eventually, help us to discern the way to healing.

Recording your thoughts about the feelings of hunger and fullness can help you to discern over time how your thoughts are shaping your overall experience. The more aware you are of your thoughts, the more aware you will become of their corresponding motivations. Consider the following questions to get you started.

- When you feel hungry, what corresponding emotions do you feel?
- When you think about eating until you're full, how does that make you feel? Why?

View each false pattern of thinking as one part of a puzzle. Discerning your overall heart motive(s) is the goal, but that happens as you put each piece of the puzzle in its proper place. The more you see the individual pieces accurately, the more you can fit them together and the clearer the big picture will become. The clearer the big picture becomes, the more you can experience growth and change.

Interactive Exercise

For the Sufferer

Learning to discern your motives is a complicated task and will likely require exploring several categories of related thought patterns. Of the common motives mentioned above, were there any you could especially relate to? Share your answers to the questions in the preceding "Discerning Motives" section. Of the four categories mentioned (food rules, extremes, triggers, and hunger/fullness) which were most applicable to you and why?

Consider the concept of inner and outer beauty discussed in 1 Samuel 16:7. What would it look like to really believe, deep down, that what really matters about us is the beauty of our hearts?

For the Helper

Your role in this exercise is one of supportive listener. You are not making judgments or asserting that you know the motives deep in the heart of your loved one. Perhaps you can ask some of the questions from this chapter and help them to think through their answers. Ask humbly and with compassion for the struggle that your friend is going through. Were there any behaviors or common motives that you think might be at play in their life? Your loved one may not agree, so don't press your evaluation. Have you observed any specific food rules in their life? What have you learned about your companion from this chapter? What have you learned about yourself?

CHAPTER 4

Dealing with Core Issues

Coming to understand your own heart and the depth of your own motivations is not easy. It can be particularly upsetting to see how deep an eating disorder goes in our own lives. If you are feeling discouraged or hopeless, don't quit. Understanding the problem is just the first step. There is great hope for change still to come. Be encouraged by the stories of others who have traveled the path of recovery. Jessica was a young college student stuck in the cycle of binging and purging and excessive exercise. She was so consumed by this dynamic that she barely finished college. Through counseling and by God's grace she was able to overcome. She is now working as a school teacher, serving in her church, and living in freedom today!

Kelly loved the Lord and faithfully served in her church, but for years she secretly harbored destructive eating habits. As she began to approach forty, the need to finally and fully deal with her eating disorder began to weigh on her. Through counseling, working intently with a dietician, and confessing her struggles to others, she found freedom for the first time in nearly two decades.

We want you to hold on to hope because the God who exposes our heart motives is also the God who delights in and is devoted to changing us and leading us, ultimately, into "the freedom of the glory of the children of God" (Romans 8:21).

Paul reminds the Philippians of the remarkable truth that God is committed to our growth, when he says, "And I am sure of this, that he who began a good work in you will bring it to completion at the day of Jesus Christ" (Philippians 1:6).

God does not leave half-finished projects. What he starts he finishes, and that includes our personal growth. God doesn't expose our motivations in order to condemn or discourage us, but to help us see how food, or thinness, or control can never satisfy us. Instead, he invites us to see how he wants to provide for us and to come to him with our needs. We can confront our motives with the truth of God's character and his promised provision. It is through confronting those motives that we can move towards greater freedom from eating disorders.

Krista's Story

I had honestly thought that my problems would be over after I transferred schools. I was convinced that I was only struggling because of my circumstances. At my old college, I was away from my boyfriend and I was stressed about grades. At my new school I knew the classes would be easier and that I could walk over to David's dorm whenever I wanted to. Changing schools sounded like a simple way to fix my issues.

But as you can probably guess, nothing really got better. New problems arose. Even though the classes were easier, I still wanted to perform with absolute perfection. Even though David was right next door, I soon discovered that he alone couldn't possibly fulfill all my social needs. I had counted on him to fill in the emptiness with his constant presence, but my expectations were overinflated. On top of all that, the campus was huge. There were ten times more students at the university than at the small college I had been attending. I found it impossible to make friends. I felt lost and alone.

All of my deep insecurities and frustrations followed me. I tried to outrun my issues, but they stuck with me because, deep down, they weren't really based on my circumstances. They had everything to do with my deeply-rooted thoughts and emotions: pride, control, perfectionism. These were the root issues that had caused me to start all the destructive behaviors. The only way I was going to actually get any better was to confront these issues.

As I mentioned, it took me years to reach a readiness to face my enslavement head-on. Our pastor did help me to confess and bring sin out into the light, but he was aware of his shortcomings, especially in the realm of eating disorders. As I mentioned in the last chapter, this is when we began assembling a team of specialists to help me. He put me in contact with a counselor who helped me to start fleshing out emotions and motivations. She worked with me to develop better strategies for structuring my life and thinking. Our pastor also pointed me toward a compassionate medical professional who assessed my physical well-being at the beginning of my recovery journey and stuck with me through the process of achieving better physical health. She was also able to prescribe medication that was helpful in stabilizing my emotions for a period of time so that I could establish traction in my recovery. Through this multifaceted team, I was able to start toward the ultimate goal of wholeness and freedom in Christ. If you need assistance in locating medical, nutritional, emotional, and psychological help I would encourage you visit the National Eating Disorder Association's website at www.nationaleatingdisorders.org.

I also found it particularly helpful to find a biblical counselor to join the team of people who were providing me with care. Many biblical counselors offer their services for a donation so this would add little to the financial strain that you and your family may already be experiencing. I benefited greatly from having someone who would meet with me regularly to sort through the mix of sin and suffering in my story by pointing me to the Word of God. We are complicated beings. Our emotions are hard to understand, and our motives are not always clear to us or others. The Bible even tells us that our hearts are deceitful (Jeremiah 17:9). But God knows all of that and so he gave us his Word as the best resource to address our situation when things go awry. A good biblical counselor can open up God's Word with you and point you to the most effective biblical strategies to help you overcome the issues that are lurking in your heart.[17]

Secondly, in order to flesh out hidden issues, I found it helpful to write out my story. I've given my testimony many times and have had to make note of different areas of my life associated with my eating disorder. I have found this writing process to be beneficial in creating a clearer picture of what is in my heart. I've included a structure that might be useful to follow as you work through the details of your struggle with an eating disorder. It is based off of the outline that I actually used to write this book. As I wrote out the details of my story to form an outline for writing, I started to see patterns of behavior in the way I dealt with life. I saw pride in the way I never asked for help nor shared about the pressures I felt as a teenager. I saw myself wrestling for control in the way I didn't want to play games as a child unless I could win. I saw perfectionism in how I always needed my outfits to match. Seemingly small and insignificant details can give us clues to reveal the deepest root of the sin that we see manifested in our behaviors. Writing also gave me the opportunity to connect my food issues with areas of suffering. I never made the connection that my eating disorder was partially in response to the trauma of my car accident until I noticed how closely these events were in the chronology of my life.

Here are a few things to think about as you write out some key points from your life story. Don't let all the information overwhelm you. You may find that you are able to see the broad picture if you write quickly without dwelling deeply on each event individually.

Childhood

- What was your family like? Who lived in your home?
- Did you have any early thoughts or behaviors that were associated with food?
- What are three key memories from your childhood?

- How was food or your body discussed in your home?
- How did you react when anything went wrong or did not go your way?
- Who was your best friend? What did you talk about?
- What was the most impactful event of your childhood?

School

- How did you feel about school? Did you like it or not? Why?
- What was your behavior and attitude like at school?
- How did you deal with failure?
- Did you have friends at school? What were they like?
- What are three key memories that you have about school?

Eating Disorder History

- What did your eating disorder look like when it first started?
- What were the first behaviors you noticed?
- How did you address the behavior once you began to sense that it was wrong?
- Did you have any rules or rituals that you had to follow? What were they?
- What is something that you feel you cannot live without?
- What is the most disturbing thing about your eating disorder?
- How did you first know that you needed help? How did you ask for help?
- What is your biggest fear?
- What circumstances would you change in your life right now if you could?

- What is your view of God in association with your eating disorder?
- What progress have you seen over the last year?
- What do you feel is the biggest obstacle keeping you from getting better?

Once I began to see the patterns in my thinking, it became easier to identify the thoughts that were making my life so difficult. Although I had confessed to those around me and I had admitted to God that I was sinning, I had not actually repented of (turned away from) my idolatrous thoughts and behavior. Some of this was merely ignorance on my part. I didn't know there was a difference between confessing and repenting. But the difference is significant.

Confessing is the first step in the entire process of removing the idols from my heart. It was only one part of the action plan that had to be carried out in order to destroy any existing remnants of the idols. I could not just identify them; I had to hate their existence and orient my trust and hope toward the God of love who alone is worthy of allegiance. I had to turn away from those thoughts and behaviors and make every effort to stop thinking or doing those things. As Isaiah instructed the people of Israel after they had sinfully turned to other gods for help, "Turn to him [God]...for in that day everyone shall cast away his idols... which your hands have sinfully made for you" (Isaiah 31:6–7). The idols could only be completely destroyed by replacing them with the one true God, by turning to him. I had to turn toward obedience and reliance on him. Repentance is a heart action that produces outward obedience, not a matter of discipline and willpower to help you behave differently. After truly repenting of my wrong thinking, I needed to turn back to God and fully trust him to forgive me and to lead me out of my suffering.

Writing out a simple story based on these questions also helped me to recognize points of suffering in the events of my life. I became more aware of situations and feelings that were hard for me to process at the time. I was better prepared to deal with them since I was out of the heat and urgency of the moment. I could take time to correctly apply biblical truth or praise God for how he had spared me or provided for me. It was also helpful to see points where I needed to give or seek forgiveness.

Three Steps Forward, Two Steps Back

David and I got married the summer before our senior year of college. We quickly wanted to have children. Because of my chaotic eating patterns, my body had not been working properly for a long time. I had not had a regular menstrual cycle in years, so I had no reason to think that I was even capable of having children at all. We ended up seeing a fertility specialist who helped to fix some of the physical issues that were keeping me from getting pregnant, and after two years of thinking it would never happen, we conceived our first child. Our future felt open, and we had no real plan for where our family would land.

While still attending seminary, David got an opportunity to serve as an intern at a church in my hometown. We were both excited about the chance to be more involved in ministry and the idea of raising our children close to our family. It all seemed to work out perfectly. We moved back from Louisville, KY and settled into a life with friends and family close by. We had another child. For once I felt like my life was falling into place. I pictured living down the street from my sister and eating dinner at my parents' house. I imagined that my kids would go to the same school that I had and be friends with the children of people I grew up with. But my plans were quickly shattered. After only five short years of living near my family, my husband was unexpectedly let go from his ministry position for reasons that were beyond our control. A whirlwind of resumes and job interviews produced an opportunity in southeast Michigan, five and half long hours away from my family and the life of my dreams.

I was crushed. I had seen real growth while we were living close to friends and family because I had been back with a stronger, more familiar support structure. I had also received more biblical teaching and counseling from our new pastor there, and I had even started studying and training to become a counselor myself. Yet some of the change I experienced was actually because of false hope. I was able to walk back into some of the roles that had made me feel successful and confident when I had lived there as a teenager, and I hated to walk away from that. While not all of this change was healthy, I did see some relief from my disordered eating behaviors. I had seemed to master the life I had at home in Ohio, but I was terrified of facing new circumstances away from the support system that had become so important to me.

We moved to Michigan, and I felt like a half-finished project. I felt as if God had shown me my motivations (achievement, success, and acceptance) without telling me what to do next. I was afraid that God had abandoned me and wasn't going to help me anymore. I worried that he had walked with me so far and then moved us to another state to let me wander. I had a support system in Ohio. I had a routine that I trusted. I thought God was taking that all away from me. But he had plans for me that I was not able to see at the time. It was in Michigan that I finally made the most progress in the fight against my eating disorder.

My husband was hired as the counseling pastor at our new church, but we both recognized an obvious disconnect between work and home. His job was to help people, but he was having difficulty helping me. Because he was so close to my situation, it had become difficult for me to listen to what my husband had to say. I couldn't stand not being perfect in his eyes. Over the years he had received extensive training and knowledge in counseling, but it didn't seem to help us through the most difficult problems within our household. Because he was part of my everyday life, I took his words more casually. His instruction, repeated over and over, became part of the background noise of my thoughts, instead of taking the foreground where it could really make an impact. I was still seeking control, battling insecurity and clinging to pride and self-sufficiency, and all of this was coming out in new and uncomfortable ways. Thanks to the tools my Ohio counselors had given me, I no longer experienced destructive eating behaviors, but I spent too much money. I held my family to unattainable standards. I couldn't make friends because I could not imagine why anyone would want to spend time with me. I couldn't form any deeper relationships because I hadn't yet reached the perfection that I wanted everyone else to see. I constantly yelled at my husband and blamed him for all my frustrations.

Things finally turned a corner when, at David's suggestion, I made an appointment with Denise, another counselor on staff at our new church in Michigan. In her, I found a counselor who helped me properly address the issues in my heart. She walked me through practical ways that I could start destroying pride and giving control to God. In this situation, Denise was a gift. Not only did she offer a supplement to David's training, she also became for me a helpful biblical filter for some of the prior counseling I had received. Instead of treating my eating disorder as a set of behaviors that needed to be eradicated, she helped me to see them as a set of beliefs and thoughts that were outwardly manifesting themselves in my actions.

Connecting to the Character of God

Denise first directed me to study the attributes of God. I had known for most of my life that I should love, obey, and follow God, but without knowing him and seeing him clearly it was hard to do any of those things. It was difficult to give myself over completely to a God that was just a blurry compilation of ideas. It was hard to trust someone I didn't even know. Seeing the love of God in the gospel gave me a deeper understanding of who is. He is not a God who is out to get me or keep track of all my wrongs, and he wasn't measuring my worth by how I performed. He is a God whose love is deep enough for me, even in my sin, that he would give his son to die for me.

Studying God's character encouraged me to develop a personal relationship with the Lord that did not involve a checklist of dos and don'ts. Because God is the essence of hope, joy, and beauty, I learned that these were things I could only truly see and experience if I got to know him better. I could not independently produce these qualities in my life. I gradually stopped trying to build my own goodness and produce my own success, and I started viewing my downfalls as ways that I could lean on God. Each of my weaknesses and struggles could be overshadowed, tended, and lovingly consumed by the love, grace, and acceptance of God.

As I continued to battle for a sense of control over my life, I was challenged to instead consider and rely on God's omnipotence. No matter how much control I gain in one area, I will always be losing control in another because I can only manage one issue at a time. I could be drastically controlling my food intake while simultaneously losing control of my family, job, and social life. Realizing that all the out-of-control aspects of my life could only ever be ordered by my all-powerful Father offered a new way of relating both to God and to my anxieties.

As I came to consider how God is just, I knew that I could no longer punish myself for my arbitrary list of rules. He alone is the true and righteous judge of right and wrong. According to God, eating a breadstick is not wrong and does not deserve the punishment of running on the treadmill for two hours. According to God's standards, it is not sinful to consume two pieces of dessert in a day, especially when they are enjoyed in a spirit of gladness and thanksgiving, so there is no need to reconcile that by not eating for three days. Because God is just, he alone decides what is *really* sin. I don't turn to myself to make those rules, and I don't need to punish myself. That is not my job.

I had used my eating disorder as a way of medicating myself. I hated how uncomfortable the world felt when things didn't go right. I hated pain. I hated the way I felt when memories of my car accident seemed to swallow any sense of security and safety I had in my life. I hated feeling any negative feelings at all, and my eating disorder promised to take all of that discomfort away. *Eat enough food to feel numb. Starve enough to master the pain.*

Exercise enough to feel that you've won something. But none of these practices offered the relief that I wanted. I wanted all of these habits to give me a predictable outcome. I wanted them to always give me a numb assurance, a cathartic rhythm that everything was going to be just as I wanted it to be. But my destructive habits often tricked me by giving me what I wanted and then suddenly dropping me into despair and loneliness and self-loathing. They promised one thing and gave me another. Only God is truly unchangeable and 100 percent reliable. Only God can make a promise and truly keep it. Only God is the same yesterday, today and forever. The positive feelings that an eating disorder can produce are only temporary, but God offers to destroy earthly sorrow with an enduring, eternal solution: the life, death, and resurrection of his Son, Jesus.

As I started getting a fuller glimpse of who God is, I began to realize that everything I needed for victory in the battle against my eating disorder was right there in him. I didn't have to fight alone, and I didn't need to look anywhere else for what I needed. His strength, compassion, wisdom, and comfort was sufficient.

If the hope of change is grounded in the trustworthiness of God, then it will be crucial for you to get to know him more. Who is he? Who does he say he is? How does he interact with humanity? Understanding this will help you respond rightly to God. The answers will help you to believe that he can truly meet your needs in ways that destructive eating habits cannot. As you begin to confront your motives and dig into heart matters, you must pair it with a growing understanding of who God is.

God tells us who he is in his Word. Your experience of God may give you particular insights and color your understanding in meaningful ways, but you must be careful not to measure God based on experience, for experiences can be misleading. You may, for example, sometimes feel as though God has abandoned you. In the midst of an eating disorder you may wonder about God's presence and compassion, but Scripture tells us that believers don't have to wonder. God has said, "I will never leave you nor forsake you" (Hebrews 13:5). We must filter all our thoughts and experiences through the truth of God's revealed Word.

God has said many things about himself within the pages of Scripture. There is far more in the Bible than we can include in this chapter. But a few key truths can help you to think about how God wants to meet your needs. As you seek to confront your core struggles, it can be helpful to consider three of God's attributes: power, love, and wisdom.

God's Power

As I touched on earlier, God is omnipotent; he can do anything he wants. The Bible describes the exercise of this power in the very beginning through the creation of the world. He simply speaks, and it comes into being (Genesis 1). He is described as having sovereign power, the right and ability to do whatever he wants, whenever and however he wants. King Nebuchadnezzar in the book of Daniel challenged God and learned the hard way that "no one can hold back his hand" (Daniel 4:35, NIV).

The psalmist declares:

Our God is in the heavens; he does all that he pleases. (Psalm 115:3)

The LORD has established his throne in the heavens, and his kingdom rules over all. (Psalm 103:19)

Whatever the LORD pleases, he does, in heaven and in earth, in the seas and in all deeps. (Psalm 135:6)

His sovereignty extends to preservation of creation (Colossians 1:17; Hebrews 1:3; 2 Peter 3:7), animal life (Psalm 104:27–29; Jonah 1:17; Matthew 6:26), seemingly random events or chance happenings (Proverbs 16:33), national affairs (Psalm 22:28; Proverbs 21:1; Acts 17:26), and our whole lives. He is sovereign over physical maladies (Exodus 4:11; John 9), over spiritual sufferings (2 Corinthians 12), and over the direction of our lives (Proverbs 16:9; 20:24; Jeremiah 10:23). God's lordship over all things knows no boundaries.

This is such an important truth because it means that God is in control. Our efforts to control the world often result in disaster, disappointment, and frustration. Sometimes they result in maladaptive behaviors like eating disorders, which, as we have seen, can be attempts to compensate for a lack of control in other areas of life. God's power means that he is both in control of all things and able to do all things. God has the right and the ability to do whatever he wants. This is both a comfort and a challenge to us.

On the one hand, God's power means that we do not get to be in control. We cannot determine what is right and true and good. He determines those standards. God also does not give us the type of autonomy we often want. We are dependent creatures who rely on him and who thrive best in community with others. He corrects us when we assert in frustration that we should be able to manage our world apart from him.

On the other hand, the fact that God is in control means that we can seek his help to make changes. We are not dependent on our own strength to quit an addictive behavior. We can count on him to help us change. His power is not just about his authority over us; it is an expression of his grace and power to help. Consider the motives you uncovered as you reflected on the previous chapters. How might the truth of God's power speak to the desires implicit in those motivations (either providing comfort or challenge)? Helpers, in what ways do you see God's power as being the ultimate form of help for your loved one?

God displayed his power most notably in raising Christ from the dead. It is because of Jesus's resurrection that we can have access to that amazing power in our own lives. Those who belong to Christ now have the Spirit of him who raised Jesus from the dead (Romans 8:11), and have replaced the spirit of fear with the power of love and self-control (2 Timothy 1:7). In Christ we have the power to live as a new creation (2 Corinthians 5:17).

71

God's Love

My struggle with an eating disorder was related, in part, to my own personal insecurity. I felt unlovable. While I knew intellectually that God loved me, that belief did not hold much weight in my life. This is true for many individuals (not just those struggling with an eating disorder). You may know that, yes, Jesus loves you, but that love does not seem to make a difference in your sense of self and your experience of others.

God is love, we are told (1 John 4:8). That is to say, God does not merely possess love, he *is* love. All that love entails is wrapped up in the person and being of God. Thus when God gives love, he more accurately gives us himself. We see this clearly communicated in the cross.

In this is love, not that we have loved God but that he loved us and sent his Son to be the propitiation for our sins. (1 John 4:10)

God's love is manifested in his sacrificial offering of himself for you. God's love is his giving himself to you and for you.

An eating disorder suggests that you are unlovable, broken, and ugly. You tell yourself that you are not thin enough, not pretty enough, not self-controlled enough. You tell yourself that you are too fat, too ugly, too unworthy. You tell yourself that you don't deserve to be loved. The list of lies you believe about yourself is long. It can be helpful to write out some of the common lies that you are tempted to believe and to investigate the ways in which God's Word responds to those lies (see the exercise at the end of this chapter). God tells you that he loves you! All these self-condemning lies are undone in the sacrifice of Christ. As that most famous of Bible verses states:

For God so loved the world that he gave his one and only Son, that everyone who believes in him shall not perish but have eternal life. (John 3:16, NIV)

God sent his Son Jesus to die for your sins. This is the ultimate measure of his love for you.

It is true, in a sense, that we are unworthy of this love, but God demonstrated the magnitude of his love when he loved us at our worst (Romans 5:7–8). Paul encourages us to regard Christ's self-giving love as expressed in the cross as a guarantee of the future generosity God intends to show us:

He who did not spare his own Son but gave him up for us all, how will he not also with him graciously give us all things? (Romans 8:32)

God already pulled out all the stops when he gave up his Son to die for us when we were his enemies (Romans 5:10). If he has already loved us at our worst, how can we imagine that we will ever reach a point where his love runs out, a point where, disgusted and fed up with us, he washes his hands of us? We can trust him to continue to love us. God's love is deeper, bigger, and more enduring than we can imagine. As you allow his love to motivate you to identify the core issues behind your eating disorder, you will discover that he will never stop loving you and that nothing can separate you from him (Romans 8:38–39).

God's Wisdom

God's matchless wisdom provides clarity to our skewed perspectives. Eating disorders have their own "logic," which sufferers tend to regard as sound and reasonable, but is often deeply flawed and unrealistic. We need the wisdom of God to help us discern the truth.

God knows what is true, right, and best for us, and he knows how to order and organize all things towards his good purposes (Romans 8:28). He knows what we need, what will help to sanctify us and conform us to the image of his beloved Son, and he knows what will bring us the greatest good in regards to what we eat and how we look. In fact, Paul says, with some rhetorical flair, that the "foolishness of God is wiser than men"—that is, our most discerning thoughts (1 Corinthians 1:25). In other words, if God could have silly or foolish thoughts, these would still be more insightful than our best and most intelligent thoughts.

God's wisdom means that he knows how to order the world and organize things to work in a specific manner (Psalm 74:17; 104:24; Jeremiah 10:12–13). That means he has determined what your body needs and what constitutes proper care of the body. You do not have the liberty to change these dynamics; they are predetermined by God's will and design.

God's wisdom also means that he has established what is true. We do not get to rewrite the boundaries of truth and false-hood or prioritize and elevate ideals that God does not value. So, if God does not value "thinness" as an ideal, then we have no right to suggest it is the most important quality to possess. If God does not permit us to be in control of all things, then we do not have the right to assert our autonomy over our dependency. If God does not establish worth based on our restraint in eating, our food rules, or our waistline, then we do not have the right to make these the determiners of personal worth. God has said what is true (1 John 4:6). His Word is called the "word of truth" (2 Timothy 2:15; Psalm 119:160; John 17:17). In multiple places Jesus himself is called the truth or said to be the provider of truth (John 1:14, 17; 14:6). Truth is found in God's wisdom.

The only proper response in light of God's wisdom is to submit to him. The Bible calls us not to lean on our own understanding but to entrust ourselves to God's wise care for us (Proverbs 3:5). Submitting to the way God has ordered the world, submitting to the truth that God has established, means letting go of our own interpretations of what is healthy, right, justified, and important. It means listening to wise and godly counselors who are speaking from God's Word and from a firm grasp on reality. The doctrine of God's wisdom ought to humble us and make us far more skeptical of our own judgments, assessments, and evaluations. Don't trust yourself; ask God and godly people for insight, clarity, and help.

Confronting Your Core Issues with the Character of God

Confronting our core heart issues is not a one-time event. It is not as though we tackle these heart struggles, resolve to believe and live differently, and then all is well. It would be wonderful if that's how change worked, but change is much more complicated. We will discuss in the final chapter the challenge of habituation and biological/psychological impact, but we want to start with the "renewing of our minds" aspect of change (Romans 12:2). For sufferers, gracious and healthy self-confrontation is going to have to become something of a new habit in your life. It will be a daily, sometimes hourly, activity. Gracefully challenging our core issues includes three key elements: (1) identifying false beliefs, (2) acknowledging the ways in which God more fully meets our needs, and (3) seeking God for those needs.

Identifying False Beliefs

There are many different ways to identify what you believe. The simplest way is to listen to the most repeated self-talk that plays in your mind. What do you most frequently say to yourself? What track is set on repeat in your mind? You may already know how you'd answer those questions, but if not, pay attention to your self-talk for a day. Write down the common or frequent things you say to yourself. Listing out your self-talk is one way to identify the false beliefs that you are adopting, because we don't often tell ourselves the truth. We may tend to overinflate our sin or underplay it. We may think too little of God or too much of ourselves. We may be overly critical of other people around us and consequently, overly proud. We may maximize our fears and minimize God's care. Listen to the tape in your head—what lies are you believing and/or perpetuating?

Another approach to identifying our false beliefs is to investigate what we believe about ourselves, God, and our situation. Identify any misconceptions, errors, or complete fallacies. Consider answering the following questions:

About Self

- What words best describe me?
- What one word would those closest to me use to describe me?
- What is my biggest struggle right now?
- What is my greatest strength?
- What makes me distinct from others?
- What do I share in common with other people?

About God

- When I think about God, what is his posture towards me (hands on hips; turned away; arms open wide, etc.)?
- When I think about God, what words would I use to describe him?
- Do I feel close to God? Why or why not?
- How does the gospel inform my relationship to God? How do I feel about this?
- When I sin, how quickly do I pray for forgiveness?
- How do I feel when I pray?

About My Situation

- What is one thing about my situation that I would change if I could?
- What is one word I would use to describe my situation?
- How does my situation impact my relationship with God and with other people?
- What can I do to help my situation? What must I ask God to do to help my situation?
- When my situation doesn't change, how am I tempted to respond?
- Can there be any good that results from my situation?

Sufferers, as you answer these questions, try to be honest and evaluate your own heart and mind carefully. Do your answers reflect the truth? Do your answers reflect how you honestly feel and think? Do your answers clash with or confirm the teachings of Scripture? Share your answers and discuss them with the friend who is working through this book with you. As you discuss, try to summarize your overall view of yourself, God, and your situation.

Remember too that not all beliefs are completely false. In most cases, we may believe things that are true but which we have overemphasized to a degree that they block out other truths that would help to color or nuance our perspective. For example, we may believe that we are horrible sinners. This is true! The Bible teaches us that we are all sinners (Romans 3:23) and deserving of God's just wrath (Romans 1:18). Yet this is not an isolated truth. The Bible also teaches us that in Christ we are redeemed and forgiven, and that no condemnation awaits those who are in Christ Jesus (Romans 8:1). So, we must hold both truths in balance, recognizing how they shape and influence one another. As you discern your false beliefs, look also to exaggerated truths that need nuance or clarification. What false beliefs can you recognize in your own life?

Acknowledging How God Meets Your Needs

Behind each lie we believe is a genuine desire for something real and important. We believe the lie that people will love us if we are skinny because we are desperate for acceptance and affirmation. We believe the lie that we should always be able to control all the details of our world because we want to feel safe and strong. There are real desires and sometimes needs that we have, and yet an eating disorder will never actually satisfy the root of those longings. Only God can satisfy our deepest longings, and so we want to look to him for help.

Sufferers, consider some of the core issues that lie at the heart of your eating disorder. What corresponding desires or potential needs might be present? Perhaps some examples will help you to think about your situation:

Core Issue	Potential Desire/Need
Control	Safety/Security
Insecurity	Love/Affirmation/Acceptance
Self-atonement	Forgiveness

In each case there is a basic desire or need that is driving the core issue and therefore driving the destructive behavior. You may be seeking to meet your own needs, but because you cannot do this sufficiently, you may pursue meeting them through maladaptive coping mechanisms.

Krista has mentioned in her own story how she was seeking security and acceptance. Instead of going to God and allowing him to provide the security she needed, she sought to create it in and for herself. This is true for all of us as it relates to all sin. Sin is always an attempt to do life apart from God, to gain happiness or escape pain on our own terms. In the case of an eating disorder we are seeking to navigate life apart from God in a very specific way. What are you seeking? In what ways have you been unwilling to seek in God what you need and want? How does God offer you what you need?

It may be helpful to write out how you can look to God to address the motives that drive your eating disorder. Identify a motive that prompts you towards your destructive habit, and identify how God responds to that motivation. So, for example, if your motive is control, what does God say about your efforts to be in control and how does he speak to your desire for protection? Discuss your answers with your helper. Helpers, be prepared to offer some input on these dynamics. Think together about relevant Bible verses that may speak to each motive.

Seeking God for Our Needs

It's one thing to know that God can provide for our needs. It is another thing entirely to seek him to meet those needs. Most of us don't struggle with knowing the right information. The reality, however, is that information does not lead to transformation. We need more than truth; we need help in the application of that truth. As we conclude this chapter, we want to focus on how we can seek God to meet our needs.

The obvious "benefit" of disordered eating behaviors is that they provide immediate results. A habitual pattern of binging, purging, or starvation works to provide the emotional relief that sufferers want in the moment. If you suffer from an eating disorder, you can temporarily feel more in control when you perform a destructive habit. You can immediately feel comfort when you gorge yourself. You may perform your habit because it "works" in some sense. Seeking God does not usually have that same sort of immediate result. Sometimes God is delighted to immediately answer a prayer with a sense of emotional comfort or relief. Sometimes he gives you just what you ask for in a tangible form. Often, however, your prayers may go on without an immediately obvious response from God. It's important not to misrepresent God's concern and care. There are those out there who will contend that with enough faith God will give you exactly what you want when you want it. There is a form of "prosperity gospel" that can appeal in seasons of crisis: if I have enough faith then God will promptly answer my prayer in the way that I most want. God, however, does not promise you that he will provide in the ways you most want, nor in your expected timeframe.

The Word of God does teach us to seek God, and it does teach us to have faith that he will provide for us in our time of need. The author of Hebrews compellingly communicates these points. So, he writes that faith means believing both that God exists and that he rewards those who seek him.

And without faith it is impossible to please him, for whoever would draw near to God must believe that he exists and that he rewards those who seek him. (Hebrews 11:6)

Faith includes believing both truths. If we don't believe that God rewards those who seek him, then we might wonder whether our request is even genuine. But, this language of "reward" does not mean that God will give us exactly what we want. The rest of Hebrews 11 details examples of faith, many of whom received rewards of blessing and prosperity. But we also read of these individuals who modeled faith in sorrow.

> Some faced jeers and flogging, and even chains and imprisonment. They were put to death by stoning; they were sawed in two; they were killed by the sword. They went about in sheepskins and goatskins, destitute, persecuted and mistreated—the world was not worthy of them. They wandered in deserts and mountains, living in caves and in holes in the ground. These were all commended for their faith. (Hebrews 11:36–39 NIV)

These are commended for their faith, and yet their prayers were not seemingly answered with immediate comfort and joy. It's important for us to recognize at the outset that seeking God does not mean using God to get what we want (control, comfort, security, acceptance, etc.). We cannot use God as a means to an end. The crisis of an eating disorder may tempt us to think and approach God that way, but God's plans, while good, are not always predictable.

If God may not give you exactly what you think you need in the moment, then what does it mean to seek God for your needs? At a foundational level, it means seeking God himself. Instead of giving you the control you want, God gives you himself and the reassurance that he is in control for your good. This is what you actually need. You need a greater sense of his presence and power in your life. In going to God for what you need, you are crying out for more of him! You are choosing to shift your focus from what you think you need to what you actually need. You are taking your eyes off of yourself and putting them on him. You are crying out with John the Baptist, "He must increase, but I must decrease" (John 3:30). You can do this through prayer, meditation on the attributes of God, reading the Scriptures, worship, and participation in Christian community.

One helpful suggestion is to read Scripture with a bent towards seeing God's character on display. Read the Psalms, for example, and ask what the verses say about God, his character and action, and his relationship to you. Or, read the stories of the Old Testament and identify the character of God on display in such stories. Study the story of Joseph and remind yourself of what God is like in action. Read the stories of Noah, Abraham, or King David. Study with an eye to see God as he is and to observe his interaction with humanity. You want to understand God better, appreciate God more fully, pray to him more earnestly, and trust that he will give you greater experiences of him as you pursue him. Ultimately, you will see the heart of God most clearly when you study Jesus in the Scriptures. Jesus tells the disciples that when they see him they see the Father (John 14:9). The whole story line of the Bible is about Jesus (Luke 24:27), so look for Christ everywhere. You need God, and he delights to give you the desire of your heart when he is the one you desire (Psalm 37:4).

Interactive Exercise

For the Sufferer

Which of the attributes of God discussed above were most meaningful to you? Why? Discuss the questions associated with each attribute. Using the template from this chapter, begin to think through your core issues and the potential needs/desires that they may correspond to. In addition, write out the ways that God may meet those needs/desires. Take time to analyze your thoughts and speak the truth of God's Word back to them. Fill out the Truth and Lies Chart below. In the first column write out any lies, partial truths, or exaggerations you are tempted to believe as the whole truth. In the second column write a biblical truth that combats that lie. In the final column, to ensure that the truth is indeed biblical, list a scriptural reference that supports that truth (see the example below).

For the Helper

Helpers, assist your companion in confronting the lies that they are tempted to believe. It is not always easy to see the truth because the lies or partial truths we believe are often compelling and convincing. Take time to assist your loved one in identifying a scriptural counterpoint to these tempting thoughts. Consider filling out the chart for yourself as well. We all struggle with believing lies, and as you seek to be helpful you have no doubt struggled with your thoughts. What have you learned about your loved one from this chapter? What have you learned about yourself?

TRUTH AND LIES CHART

Lies I Believe	Biblical Truth	Scriptural Reference
Example: I will never change	I can change because God is changing me	Philippians 1:6

CHAPTER 5

Identity

Addictive habits will inevitably raise a fundamental question about identity. The longer we engage in a pattern of life-dominating struggle, the more it impacts our sense of self. The shame and guilt we feel from certain addictive behaviors dominates our sense of who we are, casting a shadow on any other features of our character. Eating disorders, then, feel like the core of our character, not just what we do. In this chapter we hope to explore both how to untangle our sense of self from the destructive eating patterns, and how to reorient our self towards identity in Christ.

What is Identity?

Identity touches a number of different aspects of who we are, but perhaps the most dominant components are values, standards, and expressions. What we value, those essential pieces of our vision of the good life, can help to reveal something of who we are. What we value drives, at some level, what we do. We also have a set of standards by which we judge ourselves and others. We determine worth by proximity to this standard. We feel worthy when we meet our standards and unworthy when we don't; likewise, we view other people as worthy when they meet our standard and unworthy when they don't. Finally, identity relates to our self-expression. How we manifest our values and standards reveals something of who we are.

It is important to note that most of us hold some conflicting values. In this life, we will never be perfect and complete, and therefore our values will sometimes clash with one another. We may, for example, value our families, but we may also value our destructive eating habits, and so we may, on occasion, lie to our families. When our values clash, one of these principles usually wins out, revealing the deeper commitments of our hearts.

The fact that our values sometimes conflict also reminds us that our identity is often in flux. Of course, the core of who we are as children of God and as Christians does not change, but throughout life we mature, grow, and change. Our character becomes more refined as we grow in relationship with God and others in the body of Christ, and as we grow we are increasingly conformed to Christ (Romans 8:29). This means our values, standards, and expressions will continue to change throughout life. Character is always *becoming*; it is a process in translation. We are being "transformed into the [image of Christ] from one degree of glory to another" (2 Corinthians 3:18).

Krista's Story

One of the frustrating side effects of an eating disorder is that it can overwhelm and commandeer our sense of identity. I began my destructive eating habits by feeling like I was in control of them. I chose when I ate and when I didn't. I was the master and my eating habits were my servants. But as time went on, those lines between master and servant began to blur. I began to eat when I didn't want to, and I felt compelled beyond my will to then purge myself of the food I had eaten. The lines became so fuzzy at times that I didn't really know who was in charge anymore. And before I knew it, my eating disorder had completely devoured me. My identity became so wrapped up in calories and food and exercise that I didn't even know who I was. I didn't like anything else, I didn't feel anything else, and I didn't do anything else. I was my eating disorder and my eating disorder was me.

My sense of identity was an issue from the beginning. As a child I was very small. I was always thin, no matter what I ate, and people commented on it. Kids in my class would say, "You are so tiny." They'd pick me up and carry me around, "You are so light!" Sometimes they would say, "Your legs are so skinny. They look like sticks!" These comments stayed with me, congealed, and became part of my identity. In high school I was athletic and thin. People would say, "What size do you wear? You are so small!" "I wish I could eat like that and be so tiny!" I was recognized as a thin person. In college, fifteen extra pounds on my thin frame completely changed my appearance. The bones in my face weren't as defined. My jeans were tighter. My belly sagged a little through my shirts. I looked in the mirror and no longer saw someone who could be defined as "thin," and that crushed me. I didn't know who I was. I was afraid of having to decide who I was if I was no longer, "skinny," "tiny," and "small."

Then as I tried to adopt habits to deal with this extra weight I got wrapped up and overtaken by destructive "remedies." Eventually my eating disorder stole my sense of who I was and I became a person I didn't recognize. After being raised to value truth, I adopted secretive behavior and manipulated people. I became a liar. Although I admired hard work and determination, life became about quick fixes and feeling better in the moment. Deep in my heart, I valued family and relationships, but I turned down invitations and avoided conversations until I lost contact with many people who were important to me. After years of trying to eliminate food quickly and attempting to constantly take the easy way out, I became focused on the short term. My perpetual goal was to deal with the moment that was in front of me. How many calories does this have? How am I going to get rid of this meal? How will I make up for this particular thing that I ate? I had no time to think about long-term goals for my life. The endless barrage of decisions about food left me indecisive about everything else, and I simply lay down and let life sweep me away.

Eating disorders set up an unrealistic life system that always produces failure because our bodies were never meant to operate in that way. Because I followed this system, I became a person who constantly felt defeated. Because I could never arrive at the perfection that my eating disorder dictated, I started to believe that I wasn't good at anything. I stopped trying new things and I stopped taking risks. I stopped living.

We are not static creatures. Your own life is probably subject to similar ups and downs as you have experienced successes and failures. For sufferers, as you evaluate your own behavior and thought patterns, in what ways has your eating disorder become a defining feature of your self-understanding? Consider the following questions in conversation with your helper:

- What words most naturally come to mind when I think about myself?
- How have my values changed since I started engaging in my eating disorder behaviors?
- What things do I do that I would have previously never done? What things do I now excuse that I would have previously found appalling?
- What makes me "worthy"? What sorts of things determine if I had a good day?
- What areas of my life have been directly or indirectly impacted by my eating disorder? How has my eating disorder's impact on these areas of my life affected my feelings about myself?

As we come to see more clearly the way in which our destructive eating habits have impacted our identity, we want to turn to see how God gives us a new, unshakable identity in Christ.

Identity in Christ

The concept of our identity in Christ is an aspect of the doctrine of our union with Christ,[18] which refers to our being in him and his being in us. The phrase "in Christ" is a key way the New

Testament identifies those whom we call "Christians." The phrase or a variant occurs frequently in Paul's writings. In particular, the words "in Christ" appear all over the first two chapters of Ephesians, alongside variations of the phrase, giving us a good picture of what it means to belong to him. We may summarize what we discover in these chapters by saying that we are:

- Blessed *in Christ* with every spiritual blessing. (1:3)
- Chosen *in him* before the foundation of the world. (1: 4)
- Predestined for adoption by God *through Jesus Christ*. (1:5)
- Blessed *in the Beloved*. (1:6)
- Redeemed *through his blood* and forgiven of our trespasses. (1:7)
- United with all things *in him*. (1:10)
- Heirs *in him*. (1:11)
- Sealed *with the promised Holy Spirit*. (1:13)
- Spiritually alive *with Christ*. (2:5)
- Raised up *with him* and seated *with him* in the heavenly places *in Christ Jesus*. (2:6)
- Created *in Christ Jesus* for good works. (2:10)
- *In Christ* brought near to God *by the blood of Christ*. (2:13)
- Reconciled to God and to others *through the cross*. (2:16)
- A temple of God and dwelling place for God *by the Spirit*. (2:22)

The list presents us with an entirely altered conceptualization of the self. Who we were before Christ is dramatically changed when we are united with him. In relationship with Christ, we are forgiven and have our sins removed from us (Psalm 103:12), we are called as sons and treated as such, receiving blessing, promises, and an inheritance, along with the seal of the Spirit (Romans 8:15–17). Paul tells us that we are so associated with Christ when we put our faith in him that we are even united to his death and resurrection (Romans 6:1–11). He specifically states in light of this union that we are to "consider [ourselves] dead to sin and alive to God in Christ" (Romans 6:11). In other words, our whole sense of self is transformed in Christ.

Paul specifically speaks of us as a "new creation in Christ" (2 Corinthians 5:17). This means that the old ways of thinking about ourselves, apart from Christ, should "pass away." God does not think of us according to our sins, and he does not count them against us (2 Corinthians 5:19). He sees us through a different lens now—the lens of the righteousness of Christ (2 Corinthians 5: 21). In Christ, then, we do not have to be defined by what we have done! Your eating disorder is not who you are, if you are in Christ!

Furthermore, our union with Christ means that he is in us. The Scriptures teach us that Christ, by his Spirit, also indwells the believer. This indwelling by the Holy Spirit fuels our fight with sin and gives hope for the future. As Paul explains in his letter to the Romans:

> You, however, are not in the flesh but in the Spirit, if in fact the Spirit of God dwells in you. Anyone who does not have the Spirit of Christ does not belong to him. But if Christ is in you, although the body is dead because of sin, the Spirit is life because of righteousness. If the Spirit of him who raised Jesus from the dead dwells in you, he who raised Christ Jesus from the dead will also give life to your mortal bodies through his Spirit who dwells in you.
>
> So then, brothers, we are debtors, not to the flesh, to live according to the flesh. For if you live according to the flesh you will die, but if by the Spirit you put to death the deeds of the body, you will live. For all who are led by the Spirit of God are sons of God. For you did not receive the spirit of slavery to fall back into fear, but you have received the Spirit of adoption as sons, by whom we cry, "Abba! Father!" The Spirit

himself bears witness with our spirit that we are children of God, and if children, then heirs—heirs of God and fellow heirs with Christ, provided we suffer with him in order that we may also be glorified with him. (Romans 8:9–17)

Because Christ dwells in us, we do not have to surrender in the battle against destructive eating habits. We can live with confidence that, as we daily abide in Christ, he who is powerfully at work in us is able to reclaim *all* of us—our entire heart, soul, mind, and body—for his good purposes.

First Corinthians 15:57 says, "But thanks be to God, who gives us the victory through our Lord Jesus Christ." I (Krista) did not have to be forever cursed by my eating disorder. Nor did Jesus want to leave me to wallow in it throughout the course of my life. I didn't have to sit back and be okay that I had evolved into someone I didn't want to be. God gives me victory through Jesus! I don't have to be defined by what I do or what I've done. I can find complete peace in the fact that Christ identified fully with me when he died for my sins. Colossians 3:3 tells us that when Jesus died, our old selves died with him, but we were also raised when he was raised, and our lives became hidden with Christ in heaven. My broken self was hidden in Jesus so that when God looks upon me he doesn't see me alone but me united forever to his glorious son Jesus.

Not only is our identity hidden in our Savior, but as a Christian, becoming more like Christ through sanctification changes who we are. As we read the Bible, listen to biblical preaching, sing songs that pour theology into our hearts, build relationships with others, and seek to know more about God, we gradually take on the characteristics of Jesus. We become patient and loving and bold and loyal and peaceful just like him.

From the beginning of my struggles, all I wanted was to make sure that my appearance was perfect. My prayer was constantly, "Make me thin," but when I actually achieved that I felt empty and unfulfilled. It wasn't until I started praying, instead, "Make me more like Christ" that I began to feel joy. My understanding of my identity shifted to focus not on how I seemed to myself or others, but on *who* I was and *whose* I was because of Christ. This shift changed my entire outlook. I began to view imperfection not as a reason to condemn myself but as a reason to rejoice that Jesus measured up for me so that I didn't have to do it perfectly. I could rest. I could finally rest! And I could feel secure. I was free to mess up and not fear that my world was going to shatter. Not only could I rest in the fact that my identity was complete in Christ, but I could also find hope in Christ's ability to change me. The life I could live going forward was no longer filled with dread and despair but was full of an anticipation of what God was going to do next.

Hope and Help for the Fight

Settling into your union with Christ has massive implications for your struggle to overcome an eating disorder. When you are tempted to let shame have the last word, the truth that you are joined to Christ reminds you that you are not defined by what you have done! When you are tempted to throw in the towel because the battle is too hard, remember that Christ is working in you to do that which is pleasing to him (Philippians 2:13). You keep fighting because it is not in vain! When you struggle to think of what life without the broken coping tool of an eating disorder could look like, the reality of your union with Christ tells you that your "life is hidden with Christ in God" (Colossians 3:3). In Christ, everything changes!

Discuss the following questions with your helper:

- How do you imagine Christ reshaping your values? What values still need to be changed?
- How do you imagine Christ reshaping your standards? What standards (markers of worth) still need to be changed?

- How do you imagine Christ reshaping your self-expression? What elements of your self-expression still need to change?

Because we are in Christ and he is in us, we can change! Settle your identity into its proper place in relationship to Jesus and find the hope and help you need to keep changing!

Interactive Exercise

For the Sufferer

Which of the "in Christ" phrases from Ephesians (page 87) is most meaningful to you? Why? How might the truth of that phrase help to reshape your understanding of yourself? Identify additional passages of Scripture that communicate this same idea about identity in Christ.

One of the things that helped Krista reconceive her identity was beginning to pray differently ("Make me more like Christ."). Write out a prayer that asks God to help you with this goal. If you know that you struggle to want to be made into the image of Jesus, then write a prayer that asks God to give you a desire for that goal. Share your prayer with your helper.

Reflect on how this new sense of identity can empower you to live differently. Write a series of short reflections connecting this identity, rooted in your relationship to Jesus, with your response to various aspects of life (including your emotions, your eating, and your desires). For example, reflect on how your identity in Christ can help you deal with rejection, failure to keep your rules, or your desire to be thin.

For the Helper

Helpers, you too could be blessed by considering a similar prayer. In Christ, we are all being conformed to his image (Romans 8:29). In what ways have you misunderstood your identity? Write your own prayer and share it with your loved one.

Are there ways that you may be unintentionally encouraging your friend to view themselves according to a false identity (overemphasizing their beauty, intellect, talents, etc.)? As you consider this, pray with your loved one for both of you to understand your true identities in Christ.

CHAPTER 6

Restructuring Your Life for Change

It has been a long time now since I (David) have had to worry about Krista's eating habits. Most nights we sit down to dinner, and neither of us thinks about the way things used to be. We don't think about the anxiety, the tears, the arguments, or the deception. We sit with our three beautiful children and thank God for the food before us—and then we all simply eat. The freedom we have in our home now and the freedom that Krista experiences every day did not come to us overnight. That change didn't happen as a result of increased information. Change came as God gave Krista different desires. As he did, she made intentional and strategic efforts to restructure her life in order to walk in step with the new work the Spirit was doing in her (Romans 8:4–9). In this chapter we discuss what it means to restructure our lives in order to help us resist temptation and experience growth.

Krista's Story

While David was in seminary, I (Krista) took a job as a nanny. The children—an infant and a three-year-old—took to me right away. I became a second mother to them, changing their diapers, taking them on walks, drying their tears, and giving them hugs. They were my responsibility, and I felt a bit of the weight that I knew a mother must feel for her children. It became clear to me that their lives were bound up in the decisions that I made on a daily basis. I worried about them. I threw frustrated fits about them. I told stories about them. I loved them.

So the day that I found myself standing in their pantry with temptation lying before me in open rows of carbs, I stopped. I didn't tear open their Twinkies, I didn't slather their bread with peanut butter, and I didn't devour their bags of chips. Instead, I worried. I worried that if I binged, I would need to purge, and that would take me away from caring for the kids who depended on me. I didn't touch a thing. I walked away and took the kids outside while a wild animal fought within me. It was an urge that felt stronger than I could resist, but I didn't go back inside the house. We played in the yard until their mom got home, and then I went back to my apartment. I don't remember what happened after that, but the whole event stood out to me as a clear marker of my recovery. In that instance, I put others before myself, which helped me to see past my struggle and into the needs of someone else. After that, I began to see that if I could resist the lure of my eating disorder in order to care for those children, then I could resist that urge for the sake of my family, whom I loved even more. And if I could resist the urge, then I could possibly do more than that—I could take action. I could take a meal to a church member. I could call a discouraged friend. I could refrain from the rituals of my eating disorder so that I could use that time and effort in order to love others more deeply and care for their needs instead of mine. As I cared more for others, I began to care less about my self-focused insecurities. My sin began to have less power over me. Serving others became an important key to restructuring my life for change.

Consistency in Bible reading was another tool that helped me change. I grew up in church. We were *that* family who was in the pew no matter what. I attended Sunday school, went to revival meetings, forced my eyes open at sunrise services, and dragged my friends to youth group events. In each venue, I heard the Word of God. But being raised in the church was not enough. Even hearing the Bible was not enough. Learning is not the same as believing. Knowledge is not the same as faith. As my life became enveloped in struggle, I discovered that knowledge without faith is not just useless. It is worse than that; it is deceiving. Knowing Scripture without truly knowing God tells you that you are okay when you are really not. Going away to college made me face the intensity of my unmet perfectionism, my crippling insecurities, and my inflated pride. And when I tried to deal with these by resting on the faith that I thought I had, it was as if I sat down on an empty cardboard box instead of a solid chair. I rested on my history of church attendance and how many times I had heard or read the words of the Bible, but I was not truly resting on the God who spoke those words.

In my desperation to get better, I turned to the only place I knew for help: I started reading the Bible more intently. I knew that my despair was echoed in the words of the psalmists, and so every time I felt as if I could not overcome the urge to indulge in my eating rituals, I would turn to the book of Psalms and start reading. I sought God in the pages of his Word. When I was overwhelmed by shame and guilt, I knew that my God was "faithful and just to forgive [me] of [my] sins and to cleanse [me] from all unrighteousness" (1 John 1:9). I prayed to my forgiving God, filling my prayers with the Scripture I had been reading. I poured out my heart in confession with words from Psalm 51:1, "Have mercy on me, O God, according to your steadfast love; according to your abundant mercy blot out my transgressions." My desperate prayers slowly turned into conversational prayers as I got to know the Father to whom I had been crying. His forgiveness softened my heart and made me want to have a real relationship with him. After talking to him so often, he became a friend to me. I found myself talking to him constantly throughout the day.

This was not a straightforward process. It didn't happen according to an outline, with easy steps happening one after another. This process was and continues to be a gradual life-style change that weaves its way into everything I do. It is a life overhaul and as I slowly grow, it becomes less of a "have-to" habit and more of a "want-to" habit. I pursued God through reading his Word, praying to him, and studying him. He met me with a relationship that dissolved my hidden sin and made my past suffering less prominent. He worked to replace both my sinful idols and my overwhelming experiences with himself, the only true replacement. Because I learned these habits in application to these significant areas of my life, I can apply them aggressively to other issues when God opens my eyes to other areas where I stray. I was delivered from one area of struggle and can be continually delivered from many more. In this, I have found Psalm 34:4 to be acutely true in my life, "I sought the Lord and he answered me and delivered me from all my fears."

Thanks to God, I have experienced tremendous growth. Where I was once hidden in my apartment, avoiding any social gatherings, I am now eating freely at church potlucks. Where I had once felt anxiety from ordering off of a menu, I can now swing into a drive thru and quickly make a decision. Where I was once afraid to talk to anyone about what I was going through, I have now shared my story with my church and even taught a seminar at a local school. I want others to experience this same deliverance. I want to be able to help. I use to think that ten years of obsessive calorie counting and secluded food rituals was all wasted. I had deep regrets over all the things I could have done with that time. But as years went by, after I had gotten better I started to see that my struggle was something God had used to make me into who I needed to be and that it was a part of my life that I could share with others to encourage them and point them to Christ in their time of need. My faith had been tested through a trial and it resulted in an avenue to bring praise, glory and honor to God (1 Peter 1:6–7).

As Edward T. Welch wrote in his book *Side by Side*, "Those who help best are the ones who both need help and give help." [19] "Your neediness," he states, "qualifies you to help others."[20] Because I am needy and I was willing to seek help from someone else, I am now in a better position to help others. I knew that I was capable of myriads of sins. I knew that I needed to seek the Lord's forgiveness when I stumbled. I knew that I could never get better if I didn't turn to God and to others. All of this put me in a position of humility that I would not have otherwise known. That experience of humiliation turned out to be the prerequisite I needed in order to become a helper to someone else. I am qualified to help someone simply because I am a needy sinner who, through the gracious counsel and transforming power of Jesus, have been brought close in his healing embrace. Because I myself suffered, I now counsel in a humble and compassionate way (Hebrews 2:18).

As I grew, I prayed for opportunities to help others. God brought me a chance to live out what I had learned. A college student reached out to my husband for help with eating issues and he pointed her in my direction. My first counseling experience was awkward. I didn't know what to say. I left every session feeling frustrated and overwhelmed. I could have given up, but instead I looked to God for opportunities to grow. I took classes and I asked questions. I read books and I searched for answers in the Bible. I slowly started to become a helper, while still very much also needing help. Had I never needed help, I never would have been able to help someone else. But it turns out that helping others has been part of my own transformation. This opportunity will never run out, because there will always be someone who needs to be welcomed closer into the life Jesus has for us. There will always be someone who is stuck in their sin, because we are sinful people who will never be completely well until we are fully restored in Christ in the new heavens and new earth (Revelation 21:1–4). This broken world will always provide us with opportunities to help and to be helped.

Helping may look different for you than it did for me. I pursued the avenue of counseling. You don't have to go through training in order to be a help to others; this is just the road I chose to take. You may find it easier to simply seek out relationships in which to be a good listener. You may find it more within your abilities to write your story and share it with someone who would benefit from knowing that they are not alone. Or you may feel confident enough to speak to a group or join a support ministry. Whatever you do, look for opportunities to help others. It will help to magnify everything that God has been doing in your life. If you find a way to incorporate such ministry into your everyday life (such as joining a counseling ministry at your church or setting up weekly Bible study meetings with someone), you will put into place a habit that will keep you from falling back into the issues that had once bound you. A heart oriented toward loving others will be less oriented toward loving self.

The Power of Habit

The Bible is a very practical book. It was written by everyday people, experiencing both intense persecution and suffering, as well as the routine daily grind of life. The authors of Scripture write about very practical issues. They write of marriage, anxiety, death, drunkenness, and even eating. The Bible speaks to all issues, both big and small, in our lives. It speaks too about the process of change.

In Ephesians 4:17–24 Paul outlines the process of change and speaks to both removal and replacement of behaviors:

Now this I say and testify in the Lord, that you must no longer walk as the Gentiles do, in the futility of their minds. They are darkened in their understanding, alienated from the life of God because of the ignorance that is in them, due to their hardness of heart. They have become callous and have given themselves up to sensuality, greedy to practice every kind of impurity. But that is not the way you learned Christ!—assuming that you have heard about him and were taught in him, as the truth is in Jesus, to put off your old self, which belongs to your former manner of life and is corrupt through deceitful desires, and to be renewed in the spirit of your minds, and to put on the new self, created after the likeness of God in true righteousness and holiness.

Paul tells the Ephesians to stop living as the Gentiles, which is another way of saying they should stop living as those who are far from God. Christ is calling them to change. This change, however, involves both "putting off," or surrendering old sinful and destructive ways of living, and "putting on," or developing new and godly ways of living. This "putting off" and "putting on" is a practical way of living in the reality of our death and resurrection in Christ.

We have used the word "habit" repeatedly in this book. It is a useful word that expresses the complex features of our repetitive behaviors. Habits begin with choices that we make, but with enough practice, the pattern sets in and becomes less conscious. Eventually, the behavior may become our default setting, our first-choice response in any given moment. An example may help to illustrate the power of habits.

Just a few years ago we moved closer to my (David's) work. For years I had turned out of our church parking lot and gone right at the stoplight, but our new house required me to go straight at the light. For several days, I found myself turning right and traveling a mile or so down the road before it dawned on me that I had gone the wrong direction. The habit of turning right at the light was a default setting. Habits are powerful, and they increase their hold on us when they are utilized as coping mechanisms. So, if you bite your nails or grind your teeth when anxious, it is likely to happen so automatically that you don't even realize you're doing it. Even when we realize that we should change these habits, we often don't know how. How do we just stop doing it? What else is there even to do?

The process of breaking a habit is complicated by the fact that our repeated indulgence in a routine actually nurtures our love for it. James K. A. Smith speaks of our rituals and practices as "training our desires."[21] What I do is, of course, already an indicator of what I love, but the repeated practice further encourages that love. So, while obsessively working out at the gym reveals my desire for a slim and fit body, the more I work out instead of resting or going to dinner with friends, the more I reinforce that value. With every run on the treadmill I am training my heart to believe that a slim and fit body is the most important thing. It will not be enough, then, simply to stop going to the gym. I will have to develop new habits that point my heart towards new values.

The development of new habits means looking beyond merely the outward behavior—it requires a change at the heart (root) level. The values that drive an eating disorder impact a whole life, not just the dinner table. Change will require us, then, to consider our whole lives broadly and think through specific strategies that can help us. While we recognize that God alone changes us, he utilizes our efforts, our thoughts, practices, and desires. God "works in [us], both to will and to work for his good pleasure" (Philippians 2:13), and yet we are called to "work out [our] own salvation with fear and trembling" (Philippians 2:12).

Five Areas of Strategic Focus

To guide us in restructuring our life for change, we will focus on five specific strategies. Each serves as a lens through which to look at various parts of your life, and together they present a broader look at your whole life. Let's consider the five strategies and then explore them in more detail:

Avoidance. Strategies designed to help us evade obvious and known points of temptation.

Adaptation. Strategies designed to help us adjust to surprising points of temptation.

Augmentation. Strategies designed to help us develop overall character.

Amusement. Strategies designed to help us find healthy outlets for fun and relaxation.

Awe. Strategies designed to help us "see and savor Jesus Christ."[22]

Let's take a deeper look at each strategy.

1. Avoidance Strategies

One major way to help ourselves avoid giving in to sin is to avoid obvious points of temptation. A recovering alcoholic knows that one way he can help himself in the battle is by not going to the bar. While this strategy may seem obvious and clear, it is a bit more difficult with an eating disorder. We can't, after all, simply avoid all food. We have to eat if we are going to survive. So how do we develop an avoidance strategy for an eating disorder? It begins by recognizing that eating disorders are about more than food.

Avoidance strategies attempt to manage exposure to things which trigger our desire to sin. As you think about how to reengineer your unhealthy behavior, one step is to consider the types of prompts that have sparked your destructive eating habits. Look at previous exercises in this book. Perhaps one of your triggers is the scale in your bathroom. Every time you see it, you might be tempted to weigh yourself and scrutinize your size. Or perhaps that full length mirror serves to ignite temptation, or that pair of jeans you want to fit into. Perhaps you're prompted by that group of ladies who regularly discuss their most recent diet. Only you know the most obvious triggers. Share with your helper what those common triggers are, and discuss some ways to root out those specific points of temptation. What plan could you make (or unmake) to remove specific points of temptation from your routine?

Once we have worked to remove theses triggers, the battleground may shift and new prompts may develop. That's okay. This is a sign of progress; now we must seek to identify those new sources of temptation and develop the same sorts of avoidance strategies for these.

There was a time I (Krista) could not even hear other people talk about eating without sinking into my destructive thoughts and behaviors. It didn't matter if they were talking about a diet they were on and how much control they had because of it or if it was in relation to their lack of control with food and how much weight they had gained because of it, I would feel an immediate surge of panic. If I heard, "Oh, I shouldn't eat that . . . I can never eat just one," I was terrified that I would experience the same fate or that I had possibly unknowingly already started a cycle of uncontrollable eating because of something I had just eaten. At that point, I determined that if a conversation started heading in that direction, I could politely excuse myself and, for the most part, avoid any negative ramifications from it. Eventually, I could handle these conversations with a lot more discernment. I found that after discussing these types of scenarios with my counselor, I was able to formulate a plan for dealing with these types of situations. My counselor and I discussed certain situations that I might find myself in, what I might be tempted to think and feel, and the truth that I could tell myself instead. For awhile I had to avoid these types of conversations altogether, but eventually with better strategies, I could enter back into these situations able to tell myself the truth instead of listening to the lies that my mind was telling me. As these strategies became second nature, I no longer had to think about my reactions to food-related conversations.

In the beginning it felt like my counselor and I were constantly putting out fires as new triggers were always popping up. It was discouraging to think that I had dealt with one trigger only to discover that something else was a problem as well. But as I practiced the ability to put truth up against lies when I heard people talking about food, and then when I tried on new clothes, and then when I couldn't exercise because of an injury, I began to learn how to apply the strategies to various situations. I no longer had to be guided through every scenario because repeated practice had taught me how to apply a larger principle to many situations. Dealing with new triggers may just be a sign that you have been able to master certain situations and are on the path to learning how to apply what you have learned to more areas of your life.

2. Adaptation Strategies

We can only avoid so many triggers. The reality of life is that we cannot control all that comes against us. We are going to face various points of temptation over the course of our days, and we must be prepared to readjust. Adaptation strategies will help us to adjust to new conditions and respond to the unexpected in ways that honor God.

The apostle Paul models this for us in Philippians 4:11–13. We read:

> I have learned to be content whatever the circumstances. I know what it is to be in need, and I know what it is to have plenty. I have learned the secret of being content in any and every situation, whether well fed or hungry, whether living in plenty or in want. I can do all this through him who gives me strength. (NIV)

Paul has learned how to adapt to a variety of situations and, as a result, can respond to each situation with contentment in the Lord. In verse 13 he indicates how he is able to do this—it is because Christ strengthens him. We must remember that our adaptation strategies are not about our own willpower; we are still dependent upon the grace of God and yet we must work hard. We work hard because he works harder in and with us (Philippians 2:12–13).

Part of adaptation will require us to have realistic expectations. We are often surprised by temptation because we simply expect that things are going to go smoothly. Nearly every week, participants in the addiction recovery program our church runs will suggest that they have "turned the corner." They've not really done anything different; they've had a few days of sobriety under their belt, but they will claim that recovery is going to be easy from this point. Then, when temptation hits, they are shocked and unprepared to respond well. We are all going to continue to have challenges and trials ahead of us, and we will be tempted to turn again to destructive habits for comfort. If we expect this difficulty, we will be better prepared for it. Jesus tells us that "in this world you will have trouble" (John 16:33 NIV), and Peter tell us not to be "surprised at the fiery trial when it comes upon [us]" (1 Peter 4:12).

Another way to adapt to temptation is to have support at the ready. We never know when we are going to be hit by temptation, so it is best to go through life with a solid spiritual friend or two on "speed dial." Ask a few friends, family members, or spiritual mentors if you can call them in an emergency. Have their number easily acccessible in your phone so that you can call them in a moment of crisis to ask for prayer, support, or simply a way out. When temptation starts, a call to a friend can provide accountability or prayer support. When temptation becomes overwhelming and we feel that we need a way out, we can call a friend and invite them over, ask them to come get us, or encourage them to stay on the line with us until the moment has passed. Who can you ask to be on your emergency "speed dial" list?

3. Augmentation Strategies

One of the best ways we can help ourselves adapt to unanticipated threats is to strengthen our character more generally. Augmentation refers to making something greater by adding to it. In this case we want to expand the depth of our character. The stronger our overall character, the more adept we become at resisting temptation.

Eating disorders attack relationships, mental faculties (especially discernment), self-assessment, concepts of beauty, communication practices, and even hobbies. They can both weaken character and prevent the development of godly character. Addressing an eating disorder means, then, that we will have to seek to develop greater integrity, greater discernment, more realistic expectations, and more meaningful relationships. This is, of course, a lifelong process and no one ever achieves perfection in these areas. But even as we continue to work on our destructive eating habits, we can improve in these areas too. Discuss the following questions with your helper:

- What areas of your life have been impacted by your eating disorder?
- What areas of personal character development do you know you need to work on?
- Pick one area to grow in. What might be the next step to work on? You may want to brainstorm with your helper together about your ideas, and perhaps the two of you can discuss it with a wise third party for some helpful suggestions.

As you seek to measure growth in your character, remember that perfection is NOT the goal. A counseling friend of mine talks about evaluating growth in terms of frequency, duration, and intensity.[23]

As our character grows, we should see increases in our frequency, duration, an intensity of positive character attributes. Likewise, we should see decreases in our frequency, duration, and intensity of corresponding negative attributes. For example, if I am working on my patience, I should see more frequent episodes of patience, and patience that lasts longer, and the ability to be patient in increasingly intense situations. I am not likely going to see all of these at once, but I the more I work at cultivating patience, the more variations I will see. Likewise, I should see less frequent outbursts, less drawn-out episodes of anger and bitterness, and less intense moments of frustration. Again, I will not likely see all of these at once, but will see variations as I work on my patience. Evaluate yourself carefully as you work on your character, and ask for objective input on your progress.

Helpers, you will need to be an honest and clarifying voice for your loved ones. Over the years, as Krista struggled with insecurity, I have often had to remind her of how much growth I have seen in her. I have had to remind her of developments in her character, pointing out ways she would have responded sinfully in years past and how she is responding differently now. I have also had to speak truth in love (Ephesians 4:15), and help her see areas of needed growth. Your voice will be an important one as your loved one's discernment and self-assessment, especially early on, are sometimes skewed towards the negative, critical, or unrealistic.

Character development goes more smoothly when we can work on it with someone else. Helpers, identify an area where you can work on augmenting your character as well. Where do you need to grow and develop? How can you work on improving this area of your character? Discuss it with your loved one, and perhaps seek an objective third party for help in coming up with a plan for moving forward.

4. Amusement Strategies

This strategy reminds us that change will not come simply by saying "no" to every impulse and desire. We must also be able to say "yes" to healthy outlets for fun and enjoyment. Eating disorders tend to divert attention away from so many productive activities. Hobbies that were once meaningful can become forgotten or joyless. As we seek to find healthy alternatives to destructive habits, we may look to recover old hobbies, but we may also need to try something new.

Obedience to God should not be a joyless duty. God is concerned with our delight and the enjoyment of life. The Bible speaks about our joy and even encourages us to enjoy God and rejoice in the Lord (Psalm 33:1; Philippians 4:4; 1 Thessalonians 5:16). The author of Ecclesiastes, after exploring the vanity of pursuing wealth, concludes that it is right and good for man to enjoy what God gives him. He writes:

> Behold, what I have seen to be good and fitting is to eat and drink and find enjoyment in all the toil with which one toils under the sun the few days of his life that God has given him, for this is his lot. Everyone also to

whom God has given wealth and possessions and power to enjoy them, and to accept his lot and rejoice in his toil—this is the gift of God. (Ecclesiastes 5:18–19)

God gives much in life for our pleasure and joy. Paul adds his voice to this theme when he says twice in his first letter to Timothy that God has provided us with good gifts for our enjoyment (1 Timothy 4:4; 6:17). We ought to pursue healthy outlets for fun and recreation.

Addictive habits can sometimes make it feel like we have no other outlets for fun than those we have used inappropriately. The more we have indulged in our destructive eating habits, the more we have likely abandoned hobbies and other previously enjoyable activities. At this point, it can feel like the only thing that brings us any joy at all is indulging in food or restricting our diet. Finding healthy amusement may take time, but it can help us immensely to have some activities to look forward to. Discuss the following questions with your helper:

- What are some hobbies that you used to enjoy?
- What are some activities or experiences you might want to try?
- Who is someone you could ask to share these hobbies or activities?

Whatever activities you choose, don't insist that they appeal to you immediately. The activity doesn't have to be enjoyable now, but perhaps it is something you could cultivate an interest in as you engage in it over time. As you think about new outlets for fun, think of a range of both simple and more detailed ideas. Some pursuits can be exciting and serve to build anticipation, but some ventures should involve more routine parts of life. Addictive habits train us to think that only the grand and exciting can be enjoyable. Part of recovery will need to include learning to appreciate the banal activities of life as well. Perhaps you might like knitting or crocheting. Maybe you can get into photography or crossword puzzles. Maybe you'd enjoy hiking, dancing, taking an art class, or learning a musical instrument. Explore ideas with your helper. Discuss the following questions together:

- What big activities or events can you plan and look forward to?
- What simple, routine, or more mundane activities or hobbies can you develop?

5. Awe Strategies

The greatest resource we have in helping us to fight temptation is not a strategy but a person. The more we become captivated with Jesus's love, the less likely it is that we will be seduced by other "lovers" promising what only he can give. As his place in our life increases, our natural bent toward self-focus will begin to decrease (John 3:30). A vital component to the fight against an eating disorder is to cultivate a greater love for God.

To say "no" to sinful desires, we need to cultivate new desire. Negative life consequences are often not enough to compel us to stop destructive habits, nor is the inevitable dissatisfaction that an eating disorder delivers. Instead, we need to be captured by a better vision for our life than the one that an eating disorder proposes. A higher vision and a deeper love have the power to drive out the desire for our sinful and enslaving habits. In particular, we need to see and rejoice in the beauty of God and his love for us. We want to be enamored by his character, power, promises, and presence, rejoicing in what he has accomplished for us on the cross. We want to be in awe of God.

We often lose our sense of awe over God for a number of reasons. Paul Tripp has helpfully catalogued and expounded on these in his book *Awe*.[24] He describes how we allow lesser things to replace God in our hearts and before our eyes. He describes our tendency to forget God. We complain against him, love material things more than him, and sometimes we simply just choose disobedience over awe. Eating disorders often develop in conjunction with our loss of interest in God and the things of

God. We become more enamored with what food, our waistline, or our sense of control can do for us than we are enamored with God. As you look back at your own life, what are some reasons that you may have lost your awe of the Lord? When was the last time you remember being deeply struck by how amazing God is?

The Bible can help us to recapture some of that awe. Though we may often read the Bible or hear good sermons, it is possible to develop a familiarity regarding the things of God. Familiarity can breed a quiet, even accidental contempt, so that truths that should capture and compel us to respond with wonder become commonplace. In such situations, it may be helpful to look at the Scriptures slowly and carefully again, to meditate on their words instead of assuming you know them. Consider, for example, Psalm 145. Verses 1–3 tell us:

> I will extol you, my God and King, and bless your name forever and ever. Every day I will bless you and praise your name forever and ever. Great is the LORD, and greatly to be praised, and his greatness is unsearchable.

Think carefully about these words and phrases. Consider what David is saying about the Lord and about his habit of praise. Helpers and sufferers, discuss this text together. What do you notice about these opening verses? What stands out to you?

King David has been captured by a glorious vision of God. He knows something about his "God and King" that compels him to praise his name "every day" and "forever and ever." He describes the Lord not simply as "great" but as possessing a depth of greatness that can't be fully understood. So deep is God's greatness that it is "unsearchable."

Consider these next verses:

> One generation shall commend your works to another, and shall declare your mighty acts. On the glorious splendor of your majesty, and on your wondrous works,

I will meditate. They shall speak of the might of your awesome deeds, and I will declare your greatness. They shall pour forth the fame of your abundant goodness and shall sing aloud of your righteousness. (vv. 4–7)

Here David looks at God's works and marvels at all that he does. He is amazed at the "might of [the Lord's] awesome deeds." Have you considered the awesomeness of God's acts? Have you thought how amazing it is that the world exists, that we exist? Have you marveled at the lengths God went to in reconciling you to himself through Christ?

The author lists some particular characteristics of the Lord that impress him in the next set of verses. He says:

The LORD is gracious and merciful, slow to anger and abounding in steadfast love. The LORD is good to all, and his mercy is over all that he has made. (vv. 8–9)

God's mercy and steadfast love are two hallmark attributes we see throughout Scripture and most notably in the reconciliation he offers us through his Son. Where else have you seen evidence of God's mercy and enduring love in your life?

The psalmist poetically expounds God's deeds in verses 14–20:

The LORD upholds all who are falling and raises up all who are bowed down. The eyes of all look to you, and you give them their food in due season. You open your hand; you satisfy the desire of every living thing. The LORD is righteous in all his ways and kind in all his works. The LORD is near to all who call on him, to all who call on him in truth. He fulfills the desire of those who fear him; he also hears their cry and saves them. The LORD preserves all who love him, but all the wicked he will destroy.

What stands out to you about the Lord's care and kindness in these verses? In what ways have you experienced this same care and kindness?

Recover your awe by spending regular time meditating on God. Meditate on his works, his character, his promises, and his gospel. What are some other truths about God that you can focus on to help increase your appreciation and gratitude for the him?

Because eating disorders are habituated responses, change will require that we work hard to restructure our life. We must cultivate new habits in place of the old. This is only possible by the help and empowerment of God's Spirit in us. We can work at restructuring our life and responses precisely because God is working harder in us (Philippians 2:12–13)! There is hope for change, even when it requires hard work, precisely because God is changing us.

Interactive Exercise

For the Sufferer

Looking over the various restructuring strategies above, which do you think would have the most immediate impact? Why? How can you apply that strategy right now to your life? Consider the discussion questions under each category and take note of new insights and ideas you gain from deeper analysis.

For the Helper

You can assist your loved one in the development of these strategies. Discuss which strategy they would like to start with and help them think through a plan to implement it immediately. Hold them accountable over the next several weeks (perhaps by participating in that strategy too). As you grow together, help one another move on to another strategy. (See the following restructuring plan chart)

Restructuring Evaluation

Rank 1 – Most Change Needed 5 – Least Change Needed	Focal Area	What weakness does this strategy address?	New Activity to Try
	Avoidance Strategies		
	Adaptation Strategies		
	Augmentation Strategies		
	Amusement Strategies		
	Awe Strategies		

CHAPTER 7

Working Together toward Healing

As we look back over the years, it is easy for Krista and I (David) to acknowledge all the ways that we failed. It took us a long time to learn to work together, a long time to discuss issues honestly and humbly, and a long time for Krista to make progress. The slow pace is owing to our own ignorance and sin and to the generally slow nature of spiritual healing and transformation. We had a lot that we needed to learn. As we close this book, we'd like to walk you through how we learned to work together. The goal of this final narrative is that sufferers and helpers might learn sooner than we did how to work together to address destructive eating habits.

Getting Help

Talking with Krista about her eating disorder was not easy. It was awkward for us because the issues were sensitive, she was embarrassed and ashamed, and I didn't know what to say. I was also often selfishly frustrated, and I didn't want to have to spend my evening talking about her issues. So, I would sometimes insist that she seek out a counselor, mainly with the goal of simply relieving me from having to help. Although God definitely used an outside counselor to help us make progress together—and I cannot speak enough about the importance of this step—even still, Krista struggled because I (David) was impatient and a poor partner in this respect and because, for myself as for Krista, the eating disorder was simply exhausting. Spouses of those suffering with eating disorders face a unique and challenging call to suffer with and alongside those with an eating disorder. The image of bearing one another's burdens is, after all, an image of carrying a weight (Galatians 6:2). But Jesus assures that, as he helps us bear one another's burdens, we will find them lightened by fellowship with the one who also came to carry the diseases and sorrows of others (Isaiah 53:4; Matthew 8:17).

Getting an outside counselor matters because an objective third party can both say and hear difficult things. It was hard for me to hear Krista say certain things. Some of her thoughts were deeply upsetting—the despair and anger that she felt were often hard to endure. Likewise, there were things that Krista needed to hear but which were hard to accept from my mouth. My words of affirmation were viewed more as an obligation not as genuine. If I said, "You are loved," she often responded saying, "You have to say that." Intimacy can make some conversations hard. For me as a helper, my closeness to the situation made it difficult to be patient and objective. I had a vested interest in Krista getting well, and there were times where I wanted to believe that she was better instead of pressing her to do the hard work of complete recovery. On the other hand, we like to be thought of as strong and competent by those we are closest to. Krista did not like sharing all her weaknesses with me; it was just too embarrassing. We both needed to grow in these ways. It was not healthy for us to think and act that way, but it is normal. We needed help in learning to speak with and hear from one another.

This may be true for you too. You may find that conversations between helper and sufferer are difficult because you do not want to hurt one another by saying hard things. Or you may find that you are easily sensitive to comments from one another, and so you get impatient and irritated. Involving a competent counselor can help you begin to navigate some of these conversational roadblocks. Not only will a counselor be able to address issues that are too sensitive or awkward for you and your loved one to address on your own, but they may also be able to help you find ways to broach other topics.

In our case, it was David's colleague Denise who proved the most helpful. She had been counseling for about twenty years and had great experience in dealing with issues involving eating disorders. She became an unbiased and truthful source of wisdom and feedback. Denise based her observations and advice on the Word of God and on the wisdom and experience he had given her. We developed a relationship with Denise in which she could bluntly tell us what we needed to hear but she did it softly and with a great sense of care for our souls. She embodied the "faithful wounds" of a friend (Proverbs 27:6). She was able to set a plan of action for each of us individually that involved knowing God better and rooting out deeper issues of sin and suffering. Sometimes she repeated herself or told me things I (Krista) thought I already knew. *I've heard that before,* I would think. But those were the very phrases that began popping into my mind when I needed them most. During one fight with my husband I suddenly recalled her saying, "You don't have to be right." She had a way of pulling out our distinct struggles and having proper words to combat them. She also brought us together by pointing out that we each bring a different color to our marriage, as each person brings unique experiences and characteristics to any relationship. As she splotched paint onto a piece of paper and swirled the individual colors, they became a new color. That was proof to me that David is my helper for life; we are now one color and we must work together. It doesn't do any good for me to try to run away and resist.

Learning to Communicate

As we both grew, there were several important principles that helped shape our communication. Learning to discuss our struggles honestly started by moving slowly. I (David) wanted to fix the problem, and so I viewed every conversation as the solution. That put an immense amount of pressure on each conversation and on us. I learned to be patient as we dialogued, to allow some matters to go without immediate or obvious resolution. It was even okay to repeat some conversations, or to say the same things again. I learned that it was okay simply to listen and ask good questions; I didn't have to have answers.

We also learned that we needed to be more intentional about our communication. Much of our habit early on was to just hope that meaningful conversations took place organically. Since we were not accustomed to initiating deep heart exchanges or sharing our burdens (aside from complaints and rants), meaningful conversations did not just happen. Often, we would settle into routines, going to school and work, and rounding out the evening in front of the television. It was not until many years into our relationship that we decided to plan for important conversations. I (David) specifically learned that I needed to initiate check-ins. I needed to ask Krista how she was doing and refuse to settle for surface-level responses.

Ask for Help

Asking for help is not something I (Krista) enjoy doing. I would honestly rather be stuck in traffic for hours while trying to settle my screaming three-year-old. I am perpetually under the impression that I am fully capable of accomplishing everything on my own. But sometimes in life you are faced with circumstances that force you to reckon with your neediness. After giving birth to my second child, my body declined in such a dramatic way that it scared my family. I spent a lot of days laying on the couch with a blanket over me. I was weak and my joints were so painful that I couldn't move. Through various tests we found that I had drastically lost bone mass and that my thyroid was not functioning very well. Doctors put me on medication and I eventually started to gain more energy, but my joints and bones still hurt to this day. It was during this time in my life that I couldn't do anything for myself and I was forced to rely on other people to help me. I learned the hard way the value of asking for help in the small things so that when bigger things come along, I will have a team that is ready to jump into action. Because of that experience, I learned to keep a team close by. I learned that asking for help with the small things, like picking up something from the store, or babysitting kids, helps to build a relationship that will be strong enough to hold you up when you are really struggling. When I was at the lowest point of my life and didn't want to ask for help, I was left with a very small team of people. When I finally had to ask for help, that experience became a strong lesson that also woke me up to the needs of others around me who aren't, after all, all that different. Now I see my own need for community as bound up with the needs of others. The practical lesson? When someone needs you to babysit and you can, say yes. If the church needs help putting away chairs, and you are able, say yes. And on the flip side, if you need someone to move some furniture, ask! If you need to borrow some camping gear, ask! If you are struggling, speak out so that you don't find yourself struggling alone. This asking for help and helping others builds a structure that is vital to making progress.

Moving Forward

Change was slow, but eventually we could both see it happening. It was sometimes easier for me (David) to notice progress than it was for Krista. In the beginning I had to point out positive developments because she was often blinded by her own feelings of depression and despair. This is an issue in any relationship when one person is struggling and another is trying to help. The person who is deep in their problems often struggles to see things clearly. Sometimes Krista's expectations were not realistic, or she was focusing on only one type of change and therefore overlooked other evidences of growth. Over time, these small points of growth began to make a substantial difference in her life.

I noticed differences when Krista was willing to host dinners in our home. Eating in front of others had always been a nerve-wracking experience for her. When an opportunity arose for us to meet with our closest friends for dinner once a month, I wasn't sure how she would feel about it. She actually loved the idea and not only jumped on it, but she proposed to cook the first meal! Things had definitely changed in the way she related to food, though it wasn't clear exactly when this change had taken place.

I also noticed her increasing honesty with me and others. Deception had been one of the biggest areas of frustration for me in the early years of her eating disorder. There were lots of secrets and misrepresentations, sometimes even outright lies. As she grew and changed, she not only avoided deceit, but she now actually shared honestly about how she felt and when she was tempted. I recall her sharing with me once that some friends had invited her to participate in a diet that many of them were doing, and those familiar lies started to pop into her mind. She admitted that she did want to participate, but she knew that it would be unwise for her. She shared with me when she had skipped a meal or when she was struggling. This was her way of inviting accountability, and it offered me an opportunity to practice empathy and patience and to pray for her.

As David mentioned above, there was never an immediate drastic change that proved that I (Krista) was now definitively delivered from my eating disorder. In fact, I still see moments of growth that surprise me, long after I would consider myself healed and recovered. Food issues are still in the background of my heart, and so I still have room to grow and strengthen my beliefs and feelings about God, my body, and eating. The most drastic change for me has and will always be the commitment to make daily choices with my spiritual growth in mind. Because this eating disorder has been the central arena of my sin struggle for most of my life, many of my major growth choices revolve around eating. Some of my experiences may seem silly to people with a much different story, but these landmark choices helped my growth to keep clipping along at a steady pace. Do I need to always use low-fat sour cream? No. Full-fat tastes better, and

I'm not indulging excessively so I made the choice to use full-fat sour cream. And then I chose it again and again. And nothing happened. I didn't suddenly balloon to six hundred pounds, and I didn't lose complete control of all other areas of my life. When I could see that sour cream was okay, I made a choice to eat butter and have a snow cone at the fair. There are still times that I have to convince myself that a choice about food is not sinful, but I try my best to push forward, do what I know is right, and then not dwell on it. It then becomes easier to make this choice again the next time. When David and I were first married, I served obsessively low-calorie meals to my in-laws. At that time, I could only eat my "safe" food in front of people. Now, however, I add more oil to the potatoes, use a fattier cut of meat, and can actually enjoy how it tastes. Healing has been slow and frustrating, and I often need encouragement. I thank my Lord that I had friends who loved me who would sit with me when I couldn't enjoy a dessert with them—and who sit with me now as we indulge with gratitude together.

While progress towards healthy eating behavior has been huge, some of the biggest differences I noticed in my life were in the arena of spiritual health. Through this whole experience, I came to realize that, though I thought I knew a lot about God and his Word, there were holes in my faith that had serious implications for my life. I simply thought I needed to be in church and read my Bible occasionally and I would be okay. It wasn't until I was forced to use all the spiritual tools that God has to offer that I understood how important the Bible, prayer, worship, meditation, and community really are. Now I imagine my spiritual life as if I am training for a battle. When I first signed up as a soldier, I knew very little because I hadn't been given any opportunity to practice. But as I was put through the training of life's hardships, I was handed tools by those around me and I found them in the pages of Scripture. Then I could fight harder and smarter and with the strength of God in me. Every challenge I have faced has given me a new tool. Every time I mess up, I am pointed back to the Scriptures and to the one whose gracious care is more than sufficient for my weakness. And I am continually reminded that because of the saving work of Jesus, my past, present and future sin was taken care of at the cross. I no longer have to feel such loathing for not measuring up because I have been given the righteousness of Christ (2 Corinthians 5:21).

As Krista became more confident in her spiritual identity and as the Lord continued to free her from destructive eating habits, she had opportunities to testify to God's grace. Whether sharing a personal testimony in a Christian school health class, at a women's retreat, or during a counseling conference, she always points to the ways in which confession of sin, saturation in the truth of Scripture, and the grace and power of God produced change. These opportunities led us into other ministry avenues. Krista has had the opportunity to encourage and counsel others who struggle, and we co-taught a course on navigating painful pasts. Then God led us to write this book as a way to carry our ministry forward together. Writing this book has been an amazing experience that has helped us to see how different our life looks now, on this side of the eating disorder. There were lots of times where we both felt like it would never get better, never be different, but it is. Don't give up if things don't change as quickly as you want them to. We never thought we'd be here, but God is faithful.

Books are wonderful resources. We both love to read and thank God that we live in a time in Christian history when so many resources are available to help Christians navigate troubles and grow in godliness. Books, however, do not change lives. We are not naive enough to think that reading this book is going to make everything better for you and your loved ones. But we do hope that it will be one of the instruments God uses to draw you towards freedom and the abundant life he has given to us in Jesus.

As you continue to move forward, refer back to the content of this book. Look back at some of the questions and exercises and perhaps go over them again. The way is long and narrow, but don't give up hope. God is faithful, and he has been pleased to change the lives of many sufferers. It is our prayer that this will be one of the many tools that God uses in your life to "run with endurance the race that is set before [you], looking to Jesus, the founder and perfecter of [your] faith" (Hebrews 12:1–2).

A Final Word

Let us give one final word to helpers and sufferers.

Helpers

Remind yourself often that your hope is in the Lord (Psalm 33:20–22). You cannot change your loved one. You cannot predict what will happen or schedule their healing. You can't even count on this book to give them motivation to change. You can, however, count on God. He is able to help, and he cares about you and your loved one. When you are anxious, frustrated, disappointed, angry, or hopeless, cry out to him. Whatever you do, don't give up. Your loved one needs you, and with God all things are possible (Matthew 19:26). Remember your role, your limitations, and your own needs, even as you care for others.

Sufferers

Working through this material with your companion is a huge step in the right direction. Of course, this book won't fix everything in your struggle, but you should not minimize the importance of this step and the strength and courage you have shown in taking it. Remind yourself often that "he who began a good work in you will bring it to completion" (Philippians 1:6). You can count on God. Look often to him and cry out to him for continued strength. Try to be patient and kind with your loved one and keep the lines of communication open. Speak honestly with them and listen to them in return. They may be one of God's most important gifts as he brings you on the path of healing.

Overcoming an eating disorder can sometimes feel impossible, but with God all things are possible:

Now to him who is able to keep you from stumbling and to present you blameless before the presence of his glory with great joy, to the only God, our Savior, through Jesus Christ our Lord, be glory, majesty, dominion, and authority, before all time and now and forever. Amen. (Jude 24–25)

APPENDIX A

Compulsive Exercise Evaluation

Compulsive exercising is an area of significant concern. It is often overlooked because, after all, fitness is good. The problem of compulsive exercise, however, is that it goes to extremes (refusing to give the body rest, overextending the body), and it can become fatal if left unchecked. While it can develop as a separate issue, it often accompanies eating disorders.

Answer the following questions honestly, by selecting N (never), S (sometime), F (frequently), or A (always) for each question. Tally your score up at the end.

1. You judge a day as "good" or "bad" based on how much you exercise.

2. You base your worth on how much you exercise.

3. You seldom take a day off from exercise, regardless of how you feel.

4. You exercise even if you are injured.

NEVER   SOMETIMES   FREQUENTLY   ALWAYS

5. You exercise even if you are sick.

NEVER   SOMETIMES   FREQUENTLY   ALWAYS

6. You arrange work, social, and familial responsibility around exercise.

NEVER   SOMETIMES   FREQUENTLY   ALWAYS

7. You become angry, agitated, or anxious if your exercise is interrupted.

NEVER   SOMETIMES   FREQUENTLY   ALWAYS

8. Others are concerned about how much you exercise.

NEVER   SOMETIMES   FREQUENTLY   ALWAYS

9. You are usually dissatisfied with the amount of exercise you complete.

NEVER   SOMETIMES   FREQUENTLY   ALWAYS

10. You exercise to compensate for eating or for overeating.

NEVER   SOMETIMES   FREQUENTLY   ALWAYS

11. You want to stop exercising but you are unable to.

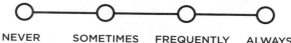

NEVER   SOMETIMES   FREQUENTLY   ALWAYS

12. The amount of exercise you do has negatively impacted your spiritual life.

NEVER   SOMETIMES   FREQUENTLY   ALWAYS

Score yourself as follows:

    1 point for every S.
    2 points for every F.
    3 points for every A.

My total score: _____

No Evidence of a Compulsive Habit: If your score is less than 10 then you may not have a compulsive exercise habit. It is important, however, to regularly evaluate yourself and make sure that you are maintaining healthy practices.

Area of Concern: If your score is between 10 and 20 then you should be concerned about the current trajectory of your exercise habit. It is time to take stock of what you are doing and reevaluate both your exercise practices and the motives behind them. If you don't act now your situation could get worse.

Compulsive Habit: If your score is between 20 and 30 then you have developed a compulsive habit that is already beginning to negatively impact your life, your sense of self, and your spirituality. It is time to take immediate action. You should seek to cut back your exercise significantly and start meeting with a counselor to help you evaluate the best way forward.

Life-Dominating Obsession: If your score is a 30 or higher then you may have entered into the realm of a life-dominating obsession. Exercise at this level can be destructive. The consequences of this behavior may already be evident in your body (physical damage and strain), social life (isolation and avoidance), and spiritual life (neglect, despair, and idolatry). You probably don't need to simply cut back exercise; you may need to cut it out altogether. This will require the careful assistance of a counselor, a physician, and close friends. Seek professional help immediately or life-threatening consequences may follow from your behavior.

APPENDIX B

Choosing a Good Counselor

Choosing a good counselor is not easy. We will give you an ideal and then help you think through some ways to navigate this situation when the ideal does not exist in your local area. Preeminent to finding a good counselor, however, is your physical safety. You want to seek medical assistance immediately in order to assess the severity of your situation and any present threat to your life.

Not all counselors are competent in the area of eating disorders, so you may have to diversify your help. You may need to seek help from a team of individual practitioners: an eating disorder specialist, a biblical counselor, and a dietician. You can learn from each and request each to interact with one another. One great option is to find a counselor who can help you focus on eating disorders and discuss some of their counseling with your biblical counselor or spiritual friend. Allow your biblical counselor both a chance to learn about the issues with you and a chance to discuss with you any directives that may not conform to biblical standards. Another option is to focus on a dietician's help with the dietary plan and work on some of those logistics while you get spiritual help at the same time.

Ideally, a counselor would provide you with the following three simultaneous avenues of care:

1. **Biblical Content.** God can use all sorts of means to help us grow and change, and because of his common grace

even non-Christian counselors can be helpful. A counselor who is particularly trained in using the Word of God, however, is a tremendous blessing. The Word of God is living and active (Hebrews 4:12); it is life-giving (Psalm 119:25). Therefore, it is invaluable to have a biblical counselor.

2. **Issue Competency.** You need a counselor who deeply understands the dynamics at play in eating disorders and who knows how to respond to these serious issues. Since eating disorders can be life-threatening you want to make sure that the person who counsels you has extensive training and more than just a passing knowledge of the issue. As you investigate counselors, ask about their experience and training in the field of eating disorders. The NEDA website provides a list of competent counselors.

3. **Compassionate Character.** One of Krista's worst experiences in counseling involved meeting with a therapist who couldn't remember her name, who suggested that she wasn't skinny enough to have an anorexia problem, and who insisted that her problems arose from a bad mother (which Krista did not agree with). This is not what good counselors do. Counselors should be good at listening, sensitive to your hurts and concerns, and kindhearted. Look for counselors who model good character in the session.

These are the ideals, but we recognize that they don't exist in every corner of the world. What do you do if you have difficulty locating such a counselor in your area?

Many of the motivations behind an eating disorder have a theological component to them. This means you need a theologically-minded counselor. Maybe that means talking with your pastor, offering him this book to guide you through the process. Maybe that means looking online to find a biblical counselor who offers virtual sessions.

There are a number of biblical counseling organizations that can help you locate counselors in your region of the country: the Association of Certified Biblical Counselors, the Christian Counseling & Education Foundation, the Biblical Counseling Coalition, and the Association of Biblical Counselors all have directories of available counselors. Some counseling centers, such as the Biblical Counseling Center in Winfield, Illinois, offer Skype sessions for those who do not have available counselors in their area.

Brad Hambrick, who serves as the pastor of counseling at The Summit Church in Durham, North Carolina has an additional guide for thinking about who to seek for counseling. I commend his guidelines provided under, "How Do I Find a Counselor Who Is a Good Match for My Needs?"[25]

For some individuals, a residential program might be the best option, particularly if you are having significant trouble making any kind of traction in your current situation. Discuss this option with loved ones.

APPENDIX C

Resources for Continued Study

Brad Bigney, *Gospel Treason: Betraying the Gospel with Hidden Idols* (Phillipsburg: P&R, 2012).

David Dunham, *Addictive Habits: Changing for Good* (Phillipsburg: P&R, 2018).

Elyse Fitzpatrick, *Idols of the Heart: Learning to Long for God Alone* (Phillipsburg: P&R, 2016).

Elyse Fitzpatrick, *Love to Eat, Hate to Eat: Breaking the Bondage of Destructive Eating Habits.* (Eugene, OR: Harvest House, 2020).

Mark Shaw, *Relapse: Biblical Prevention Strategies* (Bemidji, MN: Focus, 2011).

Mark Shaw, Rachel Bailey, and Bethany Spence, *Eating Disorders: Hope for Hungering Souls* (Bemidji, MN: Focus, 2014).

Endnotes

1. Ed Welch, *Addictions: Banquet in the Grave* (Phillipsburg: P&R, 2001), 32–36.

2. "Eating Disorder Statistics." Available online https://anad.org/education-and-awareness/about-eating-disorders/eating-disorders-statistics/.

3. "Eating Disorder Statistics."

4. T. Udo, S. Bitley, and C. M. Grilo, "Suicide attempts in U.S. adults with lifetime DSM-5 eating disorders," *BMC Medicine* 17 (2019): 120.

5. American Psychiatric Association, "Feeding and Eating Disorders," *Diagnostic and Statistical Manual of Mental Disorders*, 5th ed., 2013.

6. "Feeding and Eating Disorders."

7. Frédérique R. E. Smink, Daphne van Hoeken, and Hans W. Hoek, "Epidemiology of Eating Disorders: Incidence, Mortality Rates," *Current Psychiatry Reports* 14, no. 4 (August 2012): 406-414.

8. Carolyn Costin, *The Eating Disorder Sourcebook*, 3rd ed. (New York: McGraw-Hill, 2007), 8.

9. Carlo C. DiClemente, *Addiction and Change: How Addictions Develop and Addicted People Recover* (New York: Guilford, 2006),122.

10. Diane Langberg, *Suffering and the Heart of God: How Trauma Destroys and Christ Restores* (Greensboro: New Growth Press, 2015), 147-153.

11. For more help, see Brad Hambrick, *Burnout: Resting in God's Fairness* (Phillipsburg: P&R, 2013).

12. While this is my own evaluative form, it is based on a similar form developed by Brad Hambrick, "Online Gospel-Centered Marriage Evaluation: Listening," http://bradhambrick.com/eval-listening/#/panel/0.

13. For a more comprehensive treatment of the relationship between desire and habit see James K. A. Smith, *You Are What You Love: The Spir-*

itual Power of Habit (Grand Rapids: Brazos, 2016); see also Tim Lane and Paul David Tripp, *How People Change* (Greensboro: New Growth Press, 2006).

14. Elise Fitzpatrick, *Idols of the Heart: Learning to Long for God Alone* (Phillipsburg: P&R, 2002), 23.

15. Fitzpatrick, 25.

16. Elise Fizpatrick, *Love To Eat, Hate To Eat* (Eugene, OR: Harvest, 2005), 45.

17. See appendix B for a guide on choosing a counselor.

18. For more on this see Rankin Wilbourne, *Union with Christ: The Way to Know and Enjoy God.* (Colorado Springs: David C. Cook, 2018).

19. Edward T. Welch, *Side By Side: Walking with Others in Wisdom and Love* (Wheaton, IL: Crossway, 2015), 11.

20. Welch, 15.

21. James K. A. Smith, *Desiring the Kingdom* (Grand Rapids: Baker Academic, 2009), 59.

22. This phrase is beautifully developed by John Piper in his book S*eeing and Savoring Jesus Christ* (Wheaton, IL: Crossway, 2004).

23. Brad Hambrick, "Two Ways of Measuring Progress with Depression-Anxiety," http://bradhambrick.com/two-ways-of-measuring-progress-with-depression-anxiety/, accessed July 19, 2020.

24. Paul Tripp, *Awe: Why It Matters for Everything We Think, Say, & Do* (Wheaton, IL: Crossway, 2015).

25. Brad Hambrick, "Summit Counseling FAQs (8 of 9): How Do I Find a Counselor Who Is a Good Match for My Needs?" Blog by Brad Hambrick, August 10, 2016, http://bradhambrick.com/faq8/.